Ex Libris

Leo D. Fialkoff

ANSWER TO HISTORY

ANSWER

TO

M. R. Pahlavi

BY MOHAMMAD REZA PAHLAVI

HISTORY

THE SHAH OF IRAN

STEIN AND DAY/*Publishers*/New York

Author's Note

It is my intention that the American version of *Answer to History* be the definitive text.

M. R. Pahlavi

First published in the United States of America 1980

Designed by Louis A. Ditizio
Printed in the United States of America

STEIN AND DAY/*Publishers*/Scarborough House
Briarcliff Manor, N.Y. 10510

Library of Congress Cataloging in Publication Data

Mohammad Reza Pahlavi, Shah of Iran, 1919-80
Answer to history.

Includes index.
1. Mohammad Reza Pahlavi, Shah of Iran, 1919-80
2. Iran—Kings and rulers—Biography. I. Title.
DS318.M58413 955'.053'0924 [B] 80-52039
ISBN 0-8128-2755-4

I dedicate this book to the memory of all those Iranian men and women who have suffered and died for their country

Contents

ANSWER TO HISTORY

1

My Exile

ON SEPTEMBER 16, 1979, in Mexico, I finished the first draft of my *Answer to History,* never realizing that there would be so much more to add. Completing that earlier work had seemed like a race against time. Over the previous few months my health had grown steadily worse, with high fevers, chills, and much pain. Doctors who examined me in Cuernavaca at first guessed at hepatitis and malaria, and finally that I might be suffering a recurrence of the lymphatic cancer I had fought in Iran for six years and that had seemed dormant. Special isotopes would have had to be flown from Houston every few days for my treatment if I had remained in Mexico. Unable to reach a conclusive diagnosis, the Mexican, French, and American doctors I had consulted urged me to travel to the United States to undergo a thorough examination that only one of the great hospitals of Houston or New York could provide.

I was not eager to go. Since my departure from Teheran in January 1979, Washington had not been enthusiastic about my coming to the United States. But the Americans had always made one thing clear: I would always have access to the United States for medical treatment and assistance should my safety be threatened. These assurances had last been repeated by the American ambassador to the Bahamas when that government, under what I believe to have been British pressure, refused to extend my tourist visa. By then I no longer wanted to live in the United States. I am not a man to go where I am not wanted. But I was entitled to educate my children in America and to have access to the superior achievements of American medicine. In power, I believed that my alliance with the West was based on strength, loyalty and mutual trust. Perhaps that trust had been misguided.

In October the decision to go to New York for treatment was made. I was too sick to hesitate any longer. My staff made the necessary arrangements and on October 22 I found myself walking across the tarmac of Mexico City airport to the waiting Gulf Stream jet. The United States Consul General in Mexico City waited near the plane to prepare the necessary entry documents. I noticed his surprised expression when he saw me. This is not how he had imagined the Shahanshah, that violator of human rights and oppressor of peoples depicted by the media for so long. Clearly, I was a very sick man. Once the formalities ended, my small entourage boarded the plane. We were to stop at Fort Lauderdale for entry formalities and then fly directly to LaGuardia airport and drive from there to New York Hospital. My staff and I hoped that by taking care of the entry procedure in Florida, we would avoid the inevitable media circus in New York and the related security problems.

Nine months had passed since I left Iran, months of pain, shock, despair, and reflection. My heart bled at what I saw happening to my country. Every day reports had come of murder, bloodshed, and summary executions, the death of friends and of other innocent people. All these horrors were part of Khomeini's systematic destruction of the social fabric I had woven for my nation during a 37-year reign. And not a word of protest from American human rights advocates who had been so vocal in denouncing my "tyrannical" regime! It was a sad commentary, I reflected, that the United States, and indeed most Western countries, had adopted a double standard for international morality: anything Marxist, no matter how bloody and base, is acceptable; the policies of a socialist, centrist, or right-wing government are not.

The Western inability to see and understand clearly the grand design of Soviet expansionism had never astonished me more than in the first months of my exile. I had lived as neighbor to the masters of the Kremlin my whole adult life. In forty years I had never seen any wavering of Russia's political objectives: a relentless striving toward world domination. Moscow had time. It could wait fifty years, accept a step or two backward, deal, accommodate, but never lose sight of its final aims. I favored détente and accommodation, but not from the position of weakness and indecision that marked the policies of the American and European governments. If these policies are not reversed, Europe could be "Finlandized" in three years. Détente only makes sense if the West negotiates from a position of strength, or at least of parity. The 1980s promise to be a decade of harrowing danger. Russia will reach the apogee of her strength in 1983 and if current trends continue, the U.S. will reach its nadir, weaker than it has ever been as a world power.

Power and its application within the geopolitical structure of the world are not popular subjects for political analysis these days. Certain prominent theoreticians today speak contemptuously of the "coaling station" mentality of those who see national security as the linchpin of international discourse. But they forget that when the British navy had coaling stations for its ships in every ocean, the world was a far safer place. And even in the missile age of nuclear confrontation, conventional power remains a necessary ingredient of national policy. That power must include bases abroad and firm foreign alliances. I had believed in both. After Britain withdrew her forces from east of the Suez in 1968, I had gladly shouldered the burden of protecting the Persian Gulf. In order to meet our new responsibilities, Iran had to become a top-ranked military power, with our own bases and facilities, and the ability to protect them. I was confident that our American and British allies strongly supported these endeavors. How misplaced that confidence had been!

Even in the first months in exile I was convinced that the Western governments had some plan in mind, some grand conception or overview to stop communist expansion and xenophobic frenzy in an area so vital to the free world's welfare and prosperity. I had pondered that in Aswan in the first few days after my departure and had discussed it with President Sadat. But the hectic events of the first few months of exile, in Egypt and later in Morocco, had allowed little time for lucid analysis.

I had intended to go to the United States soon after leaving Iran, but while in Morocco I began receiving strange and disturbing messages from friends in the U.S. who were in touch with the government and from sources within the Carter Administration. The messages although not unfriendly were very cautious: perhaps this is not a good time for you to come; perhaps you could come later; perhaps we should wait and see.

About a month after my departure, the tone of the messages became warmer and they suggested that I could, of course, come to the the United States if I were so inclined. But I was no longer so inclined. How could I go to a place that had undone me? Increasingly, I began to believe that the United States had played a major role in doing just that.

This belief was affirmed in the weeks and months following my move to the Bahamas. I had gone there because it seemed a place that offered a brief vacation while not imposing any further on friends like President Sadat and King Hassan II of Morocco. I was anxious to make my own way. And although my decision to leave Morocco and visit the Bahamas had been abrupt, the move went smoothly enough, at least at first. For the journey to the Bahamas, King Hassan had kindly put an aircraft at my family's disposal. When we arrived at Nassau International Airport, we found everything had been arranged through my new advisors, former associates of my good friend Nelson Rockefeller. After greeting representatives of the Bahamian government, my family and I walked over to three waiting helicopters that were to take us to Paradise Island. I felt relaxed and confident. We landed on a golf course where the landing site had been marked with large white Xs. Our vacation home was the comfortable ocean-side villa of the Chairman of Resorts International, the owner of the compound, that included a hotel, tennis courts, and swimming pool. The three bedroom house was far from lavish, but quite adequate for our needs. After the obligatory photo session and brief chat with waiting reporters, I went in for a rest.

Our stay in the Bahamas was not an easy time. I spent much of it listening to the depressing news coming over Radio Teheran. Khomeini's revolutionary courts had swung into action. Every day stories of new atrocities flowed from my country. My friends and colleagues were being executed by firing squads. The homes of my supporters were sacked and robbed, their bank accounts looted, automobiles and personal belongings stolen. The execution a few weeks earlier of my long-time Prime Minister, Amir Abbas Hoveyda, had distressed me deeply, but it was only the starting point for Khomeini's hangmen. Just how savage they could be was driven home time and time again by vivid daily accounts of gratuitous cruelty and abuse that was meted out routinely to members of my government and their families by this so-called Islamic Republic.

When I appeared outside of my house I was mobbed by tourists. Crowds were friendly. Many requested my autograph and expressed their support for me and my family. Through speculative news stories rumors began circulating that I intended to buy into the Islands. My staff was kept busy denying one erroneous story after another.

Those were difficult weeks for me and my Bahamian vacation was anything but a holiday.

My contacts with the United States in the Bahamas were minimal. American Ambassador Schwartz called on me only near the end of my stay. My staff, however, was in contact with various other members of the embassy. Through various channels I was assured that my family was always welcome in the U.S. and that I could always go there for medical treatment. But increasingly Washington signaled some uneasiness about my presence. Perhaps that feeling was transmitted to the Bahamian government. Relations there were correct but distant. Three weeks before our visas expired my staff inquired about extending them. Officials said they would get back to us in a week. The applications were referred to higher officials and ten days before the visas expired, we learned they would not be renewed. We had ten days in which to leave the Bahamas! There was no explanation, no expression of regrets, and no further discussions with Bahamian officials.

I now have my own theories about their change in behavior. Then, they were only vague suspicions as to why we were asked to leave. Although the casino interests are the financial mainstay of the Bahamas, British influence in this former territory has remained strong, as it has elsewhere in the crown's colonies. I have a longstanding suspicion of British intent and British policy which I have never found reason to alter. With the U.S. distant and cool, and the British, as always, hostile, Bahamian Prime Minister Pindling wanted me out—despite the enormous sums I spent there for my ten weeks stay.

Two days before we were to leave, a senior official of Resorts International contacted Mark Morse, one of my aides, to inquire about my interest in remaining in the Bahamas. This kind of shifting, double-minded policy I would encounter often in exile. It had mired my last months in Iran when I never knew from one day to the next what U.S. policy was, or how reliable it was.

The immediate question, however, was where next? We did have one firm invitation, ironically from Panama. Gabriel Lewis, formerly Panama's ambassador to the U.S., came to visit me in the Bahamas and invited me to Panama. For various reasons, I was not interested at that time. However, I did send my son, Crown Prince Reza, for a visit. He met with General Torrijos and was given a brief tour of the country, including Contadora Island, which would eventually be my place of residence.

Mexico was first on my own list of preferred places of exile. While in power I had visited the country and had enjoyed its scenery and people and became friendly with the then Financial Minister Lopez-Portillo. Crash efforts were begun to explore the possibility of a Mexican haven. Several of my friends in the U.S. helped. Henry Kissinger contacted President Lopez-Portillo, as did a number of other people, including Carter Administration officials. Two days before our visas expired in the Bahamas we were invited to visit Mexico. Aides flew ahead to look for a house and found a place on a small street in Cuernavaca, an hour and a half drive from Mexico City. It was a large house that had not been lived in for several years. Lush gardens fell to a river several hundred yards below the house and rolling countryside extended along the other bank. It was a beautiful setting, although the area was thoroughly infested with mosquitoes.

On June 10 we flew to Mexico and drove from the airport in a small motorcade to Cuernavaca. President Lopez-Portillo had provided much of the necessary security. Privacy was important to me also, for I had enjoyed little of it in the Bahamas, where we were the focus of much public interest and constantly surrounded by people. My health was good at that point. The people I met were friendly, the atmosphere relaxed. I paid a courtesy call on President Lopez-Portillo and resumed a quiet social life. I now had the time and solitude to ponder the geopolitical aspects of the recent events in Iran and to reshape my philosophy on the free world's future in light of what was happening in my country.

Many friends visited, too, and helped the process. I was touched and grateful that President Nixon and Secretary of State Kissinger visited me. Both are old and treasured friends, and their visits showed how much they still cared, not only for me but more importantly for the problems we had fought together for so long to solve. I had long discussions with both men and found that our views on geopolitics still coincided, as they had during our common years in power when relations between the U.S. and Iran were so close.

My friendship with Richard Nixon dates back to 1953 when he was

Eisenhower's vice president. Our ties were strengthened both as friends and allies when he became President of the U.S. With regard to foreign affairs, President Nixon has a remarkable vision and understanding of men and events. His policies of disengagement in Vietnam and normalization of relations with the People's Republic of China were based on reason, common sense and prudence. His rigorous conception of the balance of world power gave the U.S. very definite prestige.

Before he became President, we had lengthy discussions in Teheran on many geopolitical issues and discovered we had a great deal in common. For instance, we both agreed that a nation must search for alliance with "natural allies," countries with which it will remain allied by virtue of common and permanent interests. Care must be taken to avoid doubtful alliances which are potential troublespots. A sure and solid ally is worth more than a number of partners who may weaken at the decisive moment. Richard Nixon is precisely one of those Americans who by coming to visit me in Cuernavaca has proven his loyalty to old friends.

I knew Henry Kissinger under many different circumstances, first as director of the National Security Council and subsequently as President Nixon's and then Ford's Secretary of State. He is an accomplished statesman whose breadth of understanding of American and international affairs is extraordinary. Always faithful to his principles, he served his country with an unremitting awareness of America's responsibilities for the maintenance of an honorable world peace. His superior intellect is complemented by two qualities unfortunately lacking in many of the luminaries of this world: an ability to listen and a very fine sense of humor.

We all agreed that the myth of Eurocommunism as a viable alternative to a communist takeover in the West had begun to fade. In France George Marchais had loosened ties to his Socialist partners led by François Mitterand. The move did not surprise us. Late in 1977 I had visited Poland and Czechoslovakia and in both Warsaw and Prague listened to anxious communist officials express concern that the united French left might actually win the March 1978 French Parliamentary elections. Nothing was less desirable, I was told. Communists had little interest in power shared with others. They wanted total control. Neither alliance nor coalitions such as those forged by France's Marchais, Italy's

Berlinguer, and Spain's Carillo would satisfy. Only the uncompromising stand of Portugal's Cunhal, who had closed in on power and then refused to bargain for it, was acceptable.

Communist intransigence was to be witnessed elsewhere. More than 40,000 Cuban mercenaries had begun the bitter process of carving up Africa by fomenting war, rebellion and communism from Angola to Ethiopia. Africa is the continent of the future whose raw materials are now vitally demanded by the industries of the West. They will become increasingly important as time passes—and increasingly threatened. Rival tribes disguised as nation states have riven the continent and already the dagger of dissension and race war has plunged into South Africa. China was still industrially weak. Japan unwilling to invest even a fraction of her vast new wealth in self-defense. Tokyo still relied on the American umbrella. I know from personal experience how porous that protection could be.

Meanwhile, Iran was sliding into chaos. The nation I had led to the threshhold of progress, power, and self-confidence lay torn and bleeding. A worn, fanatic old man was repeatedly telling the Iranian people how mean, miserable, and poverty-stricken they were. The women's rights I had so painfully established on a basis of dignity and pride were ground into the dust of the Middle Ages. The many projects I had begun but been unable to complete lay fallow. But then what interest could the mullahs have in the nuclear power reactors I was planning and building? The first two under construction would have added 2,500 MW capacity to Iran's power grid and their location in the northern deserts would have assured safe disposal of radioactive wastes. What would happen to schools, hospitals, universities, and other social institutions, to the new factories we were building? I had had plans to make Iran the world's largest producer of artificial fertilizer. A litany of shattered dreams!

These dreams haunted me with special poignancy the night we left Mexico for medical treatment in New York. By the time we reached Florida's Gulf Coast, it was dusk. The plane crossed the peninsula and touched down at the Fort Lauderdale airport—unfortunately at the wrong Fort Lauderdale airport. My staff had made arrangements to land at the Executive air field but instead we arrived at the executive jet section of the city's International Airport. It took the officials who had been alerted to meet us at the smaller airport about an hour to get across town to meet our plane. Meanwhile, a U.S. official approached and asked the pilot if we planned to dump garbage and whether we carried plants. He proved to be an agricultural inspector with no idea who we were.

During the two hours wait, the Empress climbed down from the plane and walked briefly nearby. I was tired and feverish and uncertain of our reception in New York. The story of my departure had been leaked in Mexico and there had been photographers at the Mexican airport. With the formalities in Florida finally completed, we were able to continue our flight to New York, arriving at LaGuardia before midnight. The plane landed in a remote part of the airport, away from other traffic. Strong security measures had been taken. New York police were everywhere. A small fleet of cars lined up on the tarmac. No TV cameras had been set up and I was grateful for that.

I was relieved to be in New York and thus assured of the best medical treatment and opinion available anywhere. We entered the cars and drove off. Originally, I had intended to stop at my sister's house in Manhattan and greet the staff there. However, when word came over the police radio that a photographer was waiting in front of the house, I decided to drive directly to New York Hospital. I was taken to two rooms on the seventeenth floor. The surroundings were familiar. Almost thirty years ago, in 1949, I had checked into those same rooms for a routine medical examination during a visit with President Truman.

The medical team that treated me, led by Dr. Benjamin Kean, who had examined me in Mexico and recommended the move to New York, came in the next morning for a thorough examination and a series of tests. Some 24 hours later, on October 24, I underwent surgery.

After the operation I issued a statement about my medical condition. In this report, I acknowledged my six-year treatment for lymphoma. In the best interests of my country, I had previously withheld this information. Recently, I had developed intermittent obstructive jaundice—the cause of which could not be determined. The question of whether the two conditions were related or not, demanded sophisticated study and analysis. My physicians at New York Hospital determined that the jaundice was due to gallstones. At 8 A.M. that morning my gallbladder and stones were surgically removed. A stone was also discovered in my common duct, which was semi-surgically removed two weeks later.

Two days after the operation I celebrated my 60th birthday with my family around me and felt myself regaining strength. The outpouring of affection for me around the world had been heartening. My rooms resembled a florist shop. Finally the overflow had to be put in a waiting room in another building and I asked that these flowers be distributed to other patients in the hospital, hoping their beauty would cheer them as well. Calls, letters, and telegrams poured into the hospital. Thousands of letters accumulated. Many were from average Americans wishing me well and offering me help. I remember one man wrote and offered me a cottage on a lake "where you'll be safe." There were many similar offers. Others urged me to "feel welcome in this country."

The friendship shown me by American citizens has always pleased and amazed me. It is in such stark contrast to media accounts, and, alas, government policy. Demonstrations against me, when they occurred, were always magnified, while shows of support were dismissed or ignored. I remember the protests during my last state visit to the U.S. in 1977 when about 50 people demonstrated against me in Williamsburg while 500 were demonstrating support for me. The media switched the numbers and asked rhetorically who had paid to bring the Shah's supporters. No one bothered to answer my own question: Who had paid the anti-Shah demonstrators to come? Surely they were paid, for it was hardly an Iranian demonstration. The crowd was dotted with black faces and blond manes, rarely found in Iran.

During my stay in New York Hospital there was little contact with the U.S. Administration. President Carter never phoned or sent a message, neither did any other high U.S. official. As I gained strength, however, a stream of visitors came to see me. I watched some television and wondered again at the media's obsession with the small groups of anti-Shah demonstrators that paraded near the hospital. As usual, little note was taken of expressions of support: one that cheered my staff involved a small plane flying up the East River floating a streamer that said "Long live the Shah."

On November 4, two weeks after my arrival in New York, militant fanatics in Teheran occupied the American embassy and seized more than fifty hostages. There is little I can say about that act of villainy, allegedly committed to "punish" the United States for offering me a medical haven. Any detailed comment would be inappropriate, even today. Nevertheless, the incident had a profound impact on my own life. Although Washington still did not communicate with me directly, the signals were unmistakable. The Administration wanted me out of the country just as quickly as was medically possible. For my part, I had no desire to stay any longer than absolutely necessary.

Thus, on November 8, I publicly expressed my willingness to leave the United States in hopes of freeing the Americans being held hostage. However, my doctors' position was that any travel for me at that time could well be fatal. I reiterated that my friendship with the U.S. remained unimpaired, and pointed out that during my reign 45,000 Americans had lived in Iran in "peace, tranquility and prosperity."

The first reaction to my statement came not from Washington but from Cairo. President Sadat dispatched Ashraf Ghorbal, Ambassador to the United States, to the hospital with an offer to return to Egypt for further medical treatment in Cairo. I was touched, of course, but unwilling at that time to impose once again on the kindness and generosity of my friend. The house in Cuernavaca was perfectly adequate for our needs. Although my visa to Mexico expired on December 9, I foresaw little trouble in renewing it. President Lopez-Portillo had told me personally on two occasions to "consider Mexico your home. You are welcome here." And according to newspapers' accounts, the Mexican government had quietly informed the U.S. that there would be no problem about my return. Again, I believed what they said. For all my growing disillusionment with the West, I still had faith.

I refused to criticize the West then and only do so today with great hesitation. It is increasingly obvious that Western policy in Iran, and indeed around the world, is dangerously short-sighted, often inept, and sometimes downright foolish. I base these conclusions upon many recent observations. To cite just one, a television broadcast of UN Security Council proceedings on the hostage crisis. There on my screen was Anthony Parsons, now the British Ambassador to the United Nations. A year before he had been Her Majesty's envoy in Teheran. I could hardly believe my ears! I can only recall the gist of his remarks. "Let these people come," and explain their revolution to us—and he meant the members of the Revolutionary Council who had already massacred so many innocent people. This was the same Parsons who told me in the fall of 1978, when I planned free elections, that if I lost them—and my throne—I would go down in history as a ruler who had lived up to his democratic ideals.

This performance was a classic example of the West's double standard. As an ally, I was expected to live up to the West's idea of democracy regardless of its unfeasibility in a country like mine. But this so-called Islamic Republic which makes a mockery of all Western ideals was cordially invited to the UN forum to educate the delegates in the new "morality" of the so-called Islamic Revolution.

As I watched Parsons' incredible performance I began to wonder if there had ever been any coherence to Western policy toward Iran beyond a successful effort to destroy me. The British hand has lain heavily on Iran for most of this century. This did not really change after the American entry. Western support of my rule had always been tempered by a need to exercise a sufficient amount of control. True, the definition of "sufficient" varied with changes on the international scene, but Western efforts to "clip my wings" go back to Mossadegh's day. They were revived whenever I struck out on my own.

The international oil companies were long-time adversaries. After Mossadegh's defeat I roused their anger by negotiating an agreement with Italy's Enrico Mattei. He had built the Italian oil company Ente Nazionale Idrocarburi (ENI) into a major but maverick competitor of the international giants. Our agreement, in and of itself, was not large but its terms were significant. Instead of splitting profits fifty-fifty as we had been doing, Mattei agreed to take only 25 percent for himself with Iran receiving 75 percent. Shortly afterwards I made the same arrangements with Standard Oil of Indiana. The fifty-fifty principle had been broken and Big Oil never forgave me. By 1959, two years after the ENI agreement, the first student demonstrations against me were orchestrated in, of all places, the United States. I suspected that Big Oil financed the demonstrations and that the CIA helped organize them. I know this sounds contradictory since both of these powerful interests had also supported my rule. But I do believe now that the West created an organized front against me to use whenever my policies diverged from theirs. I should have believed it twenty years ago when my Prime Minister, Sharif Emami, warned me that the U.S. was behind the student agitation both inside Iran and out, and was busy fomenting other trouble as well.

At the time Prime Minister Emami took the brunt of the animus, as was his legal responsibility. The U.S. wanted him out and its own man in as Prime Minister. This man was Ali Amini, and in time the pressure became too strong for me to resist, especially after John F. Kennedy was elected president. John F. Kennedy was never against me. I considered him a friend although we had little direct contact. I remember so well my first meetings with the Kennedys at the White House: Jacqueline Kennedy spoke of Amini's wonderfully flashing eyes and how much she hoped I would name him Prime Minister. Eventually I gave Amini the job. There have been rumors that Kennedy offered me a $35 million aid package as an inducement. These rumors are totally unfounded for it was Amini who obtained this money from the United States after he became Prime Minister. But he mismanaged affairs so badly that he was soon asking the Americans for another $60 million, which was refused.

After Amini's failure, I launched the series of reforms known as "The White Revolution," and for ten years the West muted its agitation against me. However, it erupted in full force again after the 1973 oil embargo and my decision to raise world oil prices. Throughout the seventies opposition mounted and in the end created a strange confluence of interests—the international oil consortium, the British and American governments, the international media, reactionary religious circles in my own country, and the relentless drive of the Communists, who had managed to infiltrate some of Iran's institutions. I do not believe that this convergence of forces represented an organized plot against me in which each part meshed with the others. But clearly all the forces involved had their own reasons for pushing me offstage. Throughout 1978, the oil consortium refused to sign a new agreement with Iran to purchase oil. This coordinated action—or inaction—had incredible significance. I believe they somehow had foreknowledge of the events that were to take place later that year. I also believe that members of the Carter Administration—especially the McGovernites in the second echelon of the State Department—were anxious to see me leave in favor of this new so-called "Islamic Republic." Their strategy, if indeed they have one, appears to assume that Islam is capable of thwarting Soviet ambitions in the region. I wonder with what? The media for its part focused on those human rights activists who deplored my rule and kept pressing for the reforms that ultimately led to disaster.

I think all this would have been easier to bear if there had been some coherent policy behind the confused and contradictory actions taken by my friends and allies. For many months I believed that such a plan existed. I have repeatedly pondered the question of Western intent and

Western policy without reaching any logical conclusion. Despite the evidence, I find it difficult to believe that the Iranian disaster was simply the result of short-sighted or non-existent policy and unresolved conflicts within the American government. Yet analysis both of the past and of events since the seizure of the hostages does not allow any other conclusion. Consider my own fate!

By the end of November 1979 the U.S. wanted me out of their country at almost any cost, and I was as eager to go. By the 27th my doctors reported that radiation treatment on my neck had been completed, and an attack of cholangitis with high fever brought under control. A stone in the common bile duct had been crushed and the particles removed. Though my doctors called the outlook "guarded," I was recovering. I wanted to return to Mexico as soon as possible.

Two days later, on November 29, the Mexicans dropped the next bombshell. That morning my aide in Mexico received confirmation from the Mexican authorities that my invitation was still valid. While making final arrangements for my arrival, he contacted my New York aide to verify the confirmation. However, in New York my aide was shortly thereafter informed by the Mexican Consul General that these plans were changed. Within less than three hours, the Mexicans had done an about face and rescinded my invitation. Foreign Minister Jorge Castenada then made the announcement official at a press conference in Mexico City. My return would be contrary to Mexico's "vital interests." He did not explain the nature of the vital interests. Press reports later quoted Mexican officials as fearing militant attacks on their embassies in the Middle East and Europe. The explanations seemed weak. I still don't know what motivated Mexican policy. They have plenty of oil for their needs and therefore had little to fear from Mideast producers. Perhaps the government hoped to play a larger political role in the councils of the Third World and feared my presence would dash that hope. I have heard accounts of a deal Cuba offered: bar the Shah and Castro would give up deadlocked efforts to win a Security Council seat and throw his support to Mexico. This theory has some plausibility. Cuba dropped out of the race and Mexico was elected.

What next? I had no quarrel with the Carter Administration about leaving, but my options were few. In addition to my own hesitation about returning to Egypt, the U.S. government feared my presence would be detrimental to President Sadat's relations with other Arab states, a groundless concern as later events would show. Panama was a possibility, as was a return to the Bahamas, although neither seemed attractive. Thus, Washington offered to let me recuperate at Lackland Air Force Base near San Antonio, and I accepted. On December 2 a U.S. Air Force plane flew us to Texas. Our departure from the hospital resembled a "getaway" scene from a 1930s gangster film. About fifty heavily armed FBI men guarded all the doors and exits and were posted in the street and the inside hallways.

Lackland Air Force Base is a training facility where a number of Iranian pilots underwent flight instruction. It is probably one of the least secure bases in the U.S. Daily, 30,000 people come and go through this military base as they would through a shopping center. There are no fences, few restricted areas. In making arrangements for my arrival the Pentagon had issued minimal instructions. The base command had little idea of how ill I was or what security requirements were necessary. When we arrived, therefore, we were put in a hospital van and driven to the most secure part of the hospital—the psychiatric ward, rooms with barred windows and locked doors. It appeared as if we had been imprisoned. The Empress grew claustrophobic. We simply could not remain in those quarters. The base commander was apologetic and friendly. He readied the visiting officers' quarters for us.

Once we were installed in the officers' quarters, things improved. General Acker, the base commander, and his top officers went out of their way to be friendly and helpful. The weather was good. My health improved. I went for walks and several times had dinner with the general and his aides. The Empress, who is a physical fitness enthusiast, enjoys tennis, and General Acker recruited some worthwhile competition for her. Some of the military on the base had served in Iran so we had an opportunity to renew old acquaintances. There was little opposition to my stay. Much of the pressure we had felt in New York began to subside.

True, we still had no place to go, but it was now Washington's problem to assist us. All the options previously explored were repeated. Austria and Switzerland were asked to take us and both again said no, even though my relations with Chancellor Bruno Kreisky of Austria had always been good and I had owned a house in Switzerland for many years. South Africa was discussed, as was Britain. Shortly after I left Iran I was informed that Margaret Thatcher had assured us we would be given asylum in England should she win the upcoming British elections. After she became Prime Minister, we were told it would be awkward for her to have us come. That position did not change.

The Carter Administration came up with an alternative, ironically one which I already had—an invitation to Panama. White House chief of staff Hamilton Jordan arrived at Lackland one day in December directly from Panama City. He had discussed a visit for me with General Torrijos and found him receptive to the idea. I discussed the proposal with my staff and decided to send my aide, Robert Armao, and my Iranian security chief to Panama with Jordan for further discussions. They visited a distant mountain resort four hours from Panama City, a location in the capital, and Contadora Island. They found the mountains were lovely, but too isolated, and Panama City too crowded and noisy. Contadora now seemed the best choice, and my aides returned with a hand-written note from General Torrijos assuring me of a warm welcome.

Jordan, joined by Lloyd Cutler, White House special counsel, then met with my staff and me to work out the necessary arrangements. My attorney, William Jackson, Dr. Kean, and my aides, together with the White House officials, finalized the plans for my departure. More importantly, an oral agreement was reached. It guaranteed full U.S. support for me should any medical and safety problems arise: Cutler and Jordan promised full White House support for the move; I would be assured access to Gorgas Hospital in the former Canal Zone, an American military installation with modern and up-to-date equipment. Dr. Kean had some doubts about how well the hospital had been maintained but acknowledged that it had once been among the finest. What is more, the Administration's men said, the Panamanian hospital at Paitilla was also first rate. And, in case of any real emergency, I would still be able to return to the U.S. Jordan assured me of President Carter's full support. The U.S. still maintained a strong military presence in Panama, another guarantee of my safety and care.

Both Jordan and Cutler were friendly and courteous throughout our discussions. The case they made for Panama became persuasive. In addition to the U.S. presence and the availability of U.S. medical facilities, Panama was sympathetic to the West. It had no diplomatic ties with Iran and presumably was immune to any threats from Khomeini. Since we had very few other options, it seemed a good solution.

After we reached an agreement with the White House, President Carter telephoned. He warmly wished me good luck and reiterated the assurances of his aides. It was the first and only time I had spoken with the President since wishing him farewell on New Year's Day 1978 when he visited Teheran.

We had but one day to pack. Before dawn on Friday, December 15, our small motorcade drove out of Lackland for nearby Kelly Field where a U.S. Air Force transport plane waited to fly us to Panama. Shortly after 7 A.M. we took off. The American promises were still ringing in my ears.

Our first weeks on Contadora were pleasant enough. The compound somewhat resembled Paradise Island. We were ensconced in a four-bedroom beach house owned by Ambassador Lewis. The island was 30 miles off the Panamanian coast in the Pacific and our house commanded a splendid view of the ocean. The heat and humidity were good for my throat, which was sore from the radiation treatments. I saw several Panamanian leaders: General Torrijos and President Royos invited me and my family to their homes and visited us on several occasions on Contadora. Both men were frequent luncheon guests on the island.

David Frost brought a television crew to the island to film an interview arranged months earlier in Mexico. I enjoyed the challenge and the intellectual stimulation which the interview afforded. Over the years I have always enjoyed friendly combat with the media. Few correspondents of major media who spent any time in Teheran ever had much trouble obtaining an interview. Talks with foreign journalists, no matter how outrageous their questions, always gave me the opportunity to explain my views on major issues. Besides, argument and debate sharpen the mind and help clarify one's own thinking. Frost is a skillful interviewer.

Too often the media, especially American, came with set notions of what Iran ought to be, rather than what it was really and more importantly what it was becoming. Iran had been propelled abruptly from the Middle Ages into today's technological world. To compare such a nation to countries with centuries of democratic traditions and histories of literacy and learning is much like comparing apples to oranges. They are simply not comparable. Glib answers to complex problems are worse than no answers at all.

America's postwar history is an uninterrupted demand that the rest of the world resemble America, no matter what the history—political, economic and social—of other nations might have been. The example of Vietnam haunts me still. Unlike the French, who had a sense of what could and could not be done, the U.S. set out to build a new nation in Vietnam modeled on itself. Ngo Dinh Diem refused to bend his policies to an unrealizeable democratic ideal as propounded by dogmatic young journalists. It was apparent that the Kennedy Administration ordered Diem's removal. It is worth noting that on the day he died, Diem was on the offensive against the communists, and that on the day afterwards the initiative had passed to the Vietcong and the North Vietnamese. Over the next twelve years the Americans and the South Vietnamese never regained it.

Democracy is an historical process that cannot be imposed by fiat, either from the bottom or the top, though my own experience suggests that gradual introduction from the top that allows time for adjustment is more effective than violent upheaval from below. My harshest critics no longer even suggest that the barbaric regime of the mullahs in Iran today is more democratic, more just, or more effective than my own. The world has rarely witnessed such a demagogic regime. In fact, I am struck by how few comparisons are made between us in the West. Few see the contrast. The Shah is put in one box, Mr. Khomeini in another, and it seems as if we ruled different countries.

By the time the Frost interview was aired in the U.S. on January 17, 1980, the early tranquility of my stay on Contadora had begun to fade. U.N. Secretary General Kurt Waldheim had undertaken his disastrous mission to Teheran and earned only contempt and ridicule for his pains. Khomeini and his henchmen never took seriously the Waldheim offer: a trade of the American hostages for a United Nations investigation of my alleged crimes. Nevertheless, Waldheim persisted for two months in chasing his illusions, giving up only when the mission he had dispatched to Teheran in March returned empty-handed to New York. They had never seen the hostages, let alone freed them. But Ghotzbadeh and the others had displayed a myriad of lies before the panel and to the world via television. It never occurred to any of the media to investigate whether or not any of the children allegedly tortured and disfigured by my police were in fact victims of other tragedies—accidents or birth defects.

On January 12, Iran's new rulers opened the next phase of their unrelenting war on history and on myself: they demanded that the

Panamanian government arrest me. The move did not surprise me but the hesitation shown by my hosts did. Instead of treating the demand with the contempt it deserved, Panamanian authorities began contributing to rumors that they were indeed in contact with Teheran, and negotiating better arrangements than the U.N. had offered. It was the beginning of a strange and ominous double game. For even as the stories circulated, the Panamanians simultaneously hastened to assure us—in secret—that there was no way I could be extradited since such extradition would violate Panamanian law. A week after the Frost interview Ghotzbadeh fired the next salvo. He claimed I had been placed under house arrest in Panama. On January 24 the Panamanian government issued an official denial. Yet days later the government waffled on the denial. There were accounts in the press of a "technical possibility" of my extradition. Again, we were given private assurances to ignore these reports.

This charade continued into February. On February 7 Panama's Foreign Minister said I was a "virtual" prisoner because I was not free to leave Contadora without Panama's permission. Gradually government pressure was increased, directly and indirectly. My staff noticed security growing lax and the tapping of our phones continued. On one occasion an aide was discussing on the telephone the high costs of our stay. The next day the Panamanians complained that too many details about money were being discussed on the telephone. A $400 tape recorder—for which we were forced to pay—was set up in the house to record all our telephone conversations. Money pressures were anything but subtle. My staff complained about bills that seemed much too high. Friends of General Torrijos let me know that Contadora was for sale and had a $10 million price. We were shown property, as we had been in the Bahamas, and again at inflated prices. But there was nothing we would consider buying. Both the White House and Torrijos had assured my staff that we would not be victimized by price gougers. Torrijos had gone out of his way to direct any complaints to his office.

Increasingly I began to sense that an effort was underway to isolate me from the rest of the world. On one occasion I flew to Panama City for a secret meeting with the American Ambassador who said he had a message from President Carter. My advisor, Robert Armao, planned to come with me to the capital, but Panamanian officials refused to let him attend. The U.S. was probably as eager as Panama not to let me be seen with my advisors—because they were American. Carter's message was that I should not worry, that everything was under control. Again "reassurances."

Pressure mounted against my American staff. Panamanian officials charged them with leaking false stories to the American papers. But they had nothing to tell. Any stories about me at that time probably were generated by U.S. government officials. Thus, after we had complained about overcharges, a story appeared in the Washington papers detailing my interest in returning to the United States. I had no such plans, of course, and certainly not after my recent experiences there. But press speculation continued and so did gentle harassment by our Panamanian hosts. I could see that Panama was not a permanent haven.

The Panamanian government was still playing extradition games with Iran. Two Paris-based lawyers, a Frenchman and an Argentinian, were employed by Khomeini to handle the legal work. They drew up a 450-page brief and journeyed around the world seeking support for this document which would have been laughed out of court in any civilized country. However, there was some doubt as to whether the Panamanians would dismiss the charges that easily. Khomeini's Panamanian lawyer argued that I could be extradited if the Teheran government promised not to execute me.

Early in March one of my American aides, Mark Morse, was arrested by Panamanian authorities and held for several hours before U.S. Embassy pressure obtained his release. He had been charged with interference in Panamanian security. In fact, authorities were angry at Morse's insistent complaints of overcharging and bill-padding.

The die was finally cast by my illness. The cancer had flared up again in February and spread to my spleen. Dr. Kean visited several times from New York to examine me and to consult with my French physician, Dr. Flandrin. Both recommended surgery and Dr. Michael De Bakey of Houston was requested to perform the operation at Górgas Hospital, the U.S. military facility in the Canal Zone. That possibility, of course, had already been discussed during the negotiations between my staff and Cutler and Jordan at Lackland Air Force Base. Then, other problems arose. The U.S. ostensibly had always held Gorgas Hospital open to us. However, the Panamanians now demanded that the operation be performed at their Paitilla Hospital.

The next act in this bizarre drama resembled a medical soap opera. My medical team and advisor met with Dr. Garcia, General Torrijos' private physician and part owner of Paitilla Hospital. Garcia was adament that the operation be done at Paitilla. Dr. Kean argued the facilities there were not adequate, that proper blood equipment and laboratories were at Gorgas Hospital. Blood would have to be taken from Paitilla and rushed to Gorgas for analysis. The discussions grew heated. The Panamanian doctors were emotional and hot-tempered and resented the foreign doctors' presence. We found it difficult to understand why any medical professional would let false nationalist pride override the welfare of a patient. Dr. Garcia bluntly stated that "we're just following President Carter's orders" and that he didn't care what we thought and that we were to do what we were told. Finally, Dr. Garcia ended the discussion with an ultimatum: "This is it. You have no choice. You either go to Paitilla or head for the airport. You are going to use our hospital."

My staff was outraged but at that moment there seemed little we could do. It was clear the U.S. wanted to keep us in Panama in order to keep playing games with Iran using me as bait for the release of the hostages. I would remain a "beloved American prisoner" on the beautiful Island of Contadora.

On March 11 we decided on the inevitable surgery. Dr. De Bakey had agreed to perform the surgery at Paitilla. Arrangements were made for moving my entourage from Contadora to Panama City. Three of my sisters flew to Panama to be with me. On March 14 I checked into the hospital.

A short time later, Dr. De Bakey, Dr. Kean, and their U.S. medical team arrived. Unfortunately, once again what appeared to be, was not. The Panamanian doctors now refused to let Dr. De Bakey operate. They claimed he was merely an itinerant surgeon and this "routine" operation could be performed by Panamanian doctors with no problems. Their pride appeared at stake. I would not be operated on by American surgeons and that was that.

I considered their attitude insane. My life was in jeopardy, and I was not about to lose it to the personal insecurities of the Panamanians. My doctors counselled against an operation at Paitilla, and agreed that surgery could be postponed for two weeks without imminent danger. The next morning I left the hospital and returned to Contadora.

At that point worldwide news reports began to detail my plight. Fortunately, Mrs. Sadat had called the Empress to express concern for my health and safety. She invited us on behalf of President Sadat to Egypt for my much needed medical care, with any doctors I desired. President Sadat would send his plane immediately.

I decided to accept President Sadat's kind offer—a standing invitation since the day I left my homeland. I have always considered him to be a noble friend and a man of honor. During those difficult days for my family and me, these sentiments were emphatically confirmed. He and Mrs. Sadat called a number of times during my stay in Panama. The message was always the same: "Why don't you come to Egypt? You are welcome here."

On March 21, Hamilton Jordan arrived in Panama. He telephoned on arrival to say that he was coming to see me. However, Jordan never came. At the same time, he contacted Lloyd Cutler who later flew to Panama with Arnold Raphel, a top aide to U.S. Secretary of State Vance. Upon his arrival in Panama, Cutler called to inquire if he could come to Contadora with a message from President Carter. We agreed, even though I knew that the Empress had already spoken with Mrs. Sadat and indicated my interest in moving to Egypt.

When Cutler arrived he insisted on seeing me without my aides present. I reluctantly agreed. I had dealt with Cutler during our Lackland negotiations, where I had found him a man of substance and tact, sure-footed in the byways of diplomatic intercourse. Now in Contadora he outlined the U.S. position with skill and detachment. My trip to Egypt, he said, could endanger Sadat's position in the Arab world, particularly the Mideast peace process. Houston was a possibility for my surgery, of course. The terms of the Lackland agreement had been specific on that point. Nevertheless, any such move during the delicate negotiations now underway could endanger resolution of the hostage crisis. The best solution, clearly, for Carter, was for me to remain in Panama. Now the concessions came quickly. Of course, the operation could be performed at Gorgas; Panamanian doctors were anxious to apologize to Dr. De Bakey. Cutler was persuasive but my decision was virtually made. Still, I agreed to consider his proposal and to see him again the next morning.

I did not seriously consider the American offers. For the last year and a half, American promises had not been worth very much. They had already cost me my throne and any further trust in them could well mean my life. When Cutler returned to my house the next morning he looked at our packed bags and understood. He did not bother trying to change my mind. Instead, he called the White House to discuss the necessary logistics. He suggested it would be wiser to use a U.S. chartered plane than to wait for Sadat's aircraft with its refueling and landing rights' questions. More calls followed. Cutler and his aides managed to charter an aircraft. The plane would meet us at Panama City International Airport.

After my decision to leave had been made, Panamanian demeanor changed. They were extremely helpful. Guards were now eager to assist us. Medically, time was of the essence: I was running a fever; my blood count was dangerously low; the blood platelet count dropped to less than 10 percent of normal. Thus, the trans-Atlantic flight would be risky, for if I cut myself at so high an altitude, I might well bleed to death.

We boarded the plane in Panama City. It was a long, uncomfortable flight, for the seats were narrow and cramped. We landed in the Azores to refuel. A Portuguese general and the American consul were waiting at the airport. Though sick and feverish, I rose, straightened my clothes and prepared to receive them, as protocol required.

Finally we landed in Cairo where President Sadat and Mrs. Sadat waited to greet us in the bright sunshine. An honor guard was posted behind them. I walked from the plane to President Sadat and his wife and warmly embraced him.

"Thank God you're safe," Sadat said, and I was safe indeed.

From the airport we flew by helicopter to Maadi Military Hospital on the Nile just outside Cairo. Doctors began at once to work on bringing down my temperature and building up my blood count. A few days later Dr. De Bakey and his medical team arrived in Cairo with their sophisticated medical equipment. Surgery was immediately necessary. X-rays revealed that my spleen was dangerously enlarged.

The surgery was performed on March 28. The removed, cancerous spleen weighed four-and-a-half pounds and resembled an oversized football. A normal spleen is the size of a man's fist.

When I was finally well enough to leave the hospital I joined my family in the Koubbeh Palace, six miles north of Cairo. This is the Egyptian residence for all visiting heads of State. It is set in the midst of a large park with fruit trees and gardens, encircled by a wall and well secured. This lovely home offered the first peace, quiet, and security we have known since leaving Iran. Its serene beauty has been a source of strength during my convalescence. Not since my stay in Mexico have I enjoyed such time for reflection and thought.

Of course, I continue to focus on events in my homeland, past and present. Certainly, I had made mistakes in Iran. However, I cannot believe they formed the basis for my downfall. They were rectifiable with time. My country stood on the verge of becoming a Great Civilization.

The forces against me, however, proved stronger, although they were gathered without unified motive or larger purpose.

Much of the opposition aroused in the West seems to have been triggered by ignorance, and a warped view of what Iran should be. The West has never understood my country. We were ignored for centuries. When we re-entered modern consciousness, it was only as a geographic cross-roads. We were merely a guardian of trade routes to the East, a savage and barbaric land of no intrinsic worth, whose importance lay in political realities. I have never denied those realities but have never understood British and American inability to recognize Iran as a truly independent nation. We live in that trapezoid of land linking the Near East to India and we are the Western wedge against Russia's centuries-old dream of warm water ports in the Persian Gulf and the Indian Ocean.

Part of the answer, I think, lies in the West's lack of interest in Iran's history and its failure to understand the differences between Persia, both ancient and modern, and itself. My own answer to history, therefore, must begin with the history of my country, the 3,000 years of Persian civilization that, misunderstood, has led to the defeat of Iran's attempt to enter the twentieth century, perhaps presaging an even greater defeat of the countries I considered friends and allies.

2

Lessons of the Past

OURS IS A VERY old country: the history of Persia goes back into the mists of time. Situated in that part of the Middle East which was the cradle of the great Western civilizations, we find ourselves at the crossroads which unite Europe and Asia, the Indian sub-continent and Africa. Our shores are washed by three seas—the Caspian to the north, the Persian Gulf to the southwest and the Gulf of Oman to the south—and we are only separated by Syria and Iraq from the Mediterranean, which was for centuries the center of the civilized world. This is the strength of our position. It allowed us, during the great moments of our history, to conquer, trade with, influence and civilize neighboring countries.

The weakness of our position is that the center of Iran is a vast plateau, on a northwest-southeast axis, with steppes and salt deserts. The plateau is surrounded on all sides by chains of mountains: the Elburz mountains more or less cover the northern frontier, the Zagros mountains lie to the west and the Baluchistan mountains to the southeast. With the exception of a few large towns (Isfahan, Kerman) the center of our country is empty and barren, and the population, activity, wealth and culture are concentrated in the surrounding provinces. That is why throughout the centuries Persia had as its capital one or the other of the great peripheral cities. Before Teheran, there were during the period of the Persian Empire, Susa, Ectabana, Persepolis and Ctesiphon, and during the Safavid period, Tabriz and Ardebil in Azerbaijan and later Isfahan, which, as a large oasis in the center of the country with unique geographical features, was an exception.

During our greatest eras, the energy, ambition, intelligence and sometimes the firm wisdom of a single leader kept us united. Other epochs were, on the contrary, marked by attacks, launched either openly or not for foreign interests, aggravated by internal complicity more or less conscious and more or less organized.

A brief review of these legendary events will make it easier to understand the meaning and the repercussions of the main episodes of a history which for the most part remains unknown.

Under the impetus of two groups of Indo-Europeans, the Medes and the Persians, we initially emerged as the victors of the peoples who for two thousand years had been quarrelling over Mesopotamia. The Achaemenid dynasty (559–330 B.C.) created the greatest Empire yet known—from the Black Sea to Central Asia and from India to Libya.

It was also the world's first real empire in which one ruler governed many different peoples. In order to make this innovation possible, the Persians divided the Empire into provinces, each under a "satrap," who was a provincial governor. They used signal stations and even a visual telegraph system: semaphor beacons erected on mountain peaks which allowed messages to be passed rapidly from one end of the Empire to the other. They also worked out monetary systems and public finance, and standardized weights and measures. Thus, Persia taught the ancient world how to govern and administer a vast empire. Rome merely imitated Persia and frequently copied her methods.

The founder of this Empire, Cyrus, deserves to be called "The Great" because he founded it on tolerance and justice. As a conqueror he should be considered the first advocate of human rights. He was the first in the ancient world to publish a charter which can be described as liberal: it freed prisoners of war and left them their land; conquered nations maintained their rights and their customs, for their laws and their religion were respected by the central power. Cyrus not only pardoned his valiant enemies, but he did not hesitate to entrust them with important responsibilities. Thus he can be deemed the liberator of peoples. This policy conformed to the Persian character. It was the policy of all sovereigns for whom peace made it possible to institute a moral order: Persia became known as a land where the persecuted might take asylum.

Cyrus II the Great, Darius and Xerxes are our hero-kings; they continued their march in works of literature and in the fine arts. Europeans have, however, mostly been taught that Darius was beaten at Marathon and Xerxes in a sea battle at Salamis (480 B.C.) These moving victories by a lesser power over a greater, frequently lead people to forget that Persia later became mistress of the Aegean Sea (394 B.C.).

The Archaemenid decline ended in a unique phenomenon: Alexander of Macedon (356–323 B.C.). He took possession of the whole of Darius' empire—with the exception of the Pontus and Chorasmia—and extended it slightly to the northeast by pushing the frontier to the river, Syr Darya. Far from carving up the Empire or exploiting it for the benefit of Greece, he imitated Cyrus, took his place and made Persia his own empire.

The carving up happened after his death (323 B.C.) and, contrary to what can be read in most Western history books, Persia was not influenced by Greek culture, although we still have a charming little Greek statue in a museum. In fact, Alexander espoused the Persian civilization. This is a phenomenon which recurred with subsequent conquerors: the Persians submitted to them but they preserved their own culture and imposed it on their victors.

Two hundred and fifty years before Christ, the Parthians imposed the Arsacid dynasty (250 B.C.– A.D. 224) which was to end almost five centuries later with the victory of the Persian Ardashir over Artabanus. The Sassanid dynasty (A.D. 224-651) was thus founded in opposition to the Parthians and to Rome. Ardashir had been the guardian of the temple of Zoroaster. The empire which he founded stretched from the Indus and the Syr Darya to the southern shores of the Persian Gulf. It played two important roles in world history—one political and the other cultural.

The Persian Empire was the first barrier against the savage or half-savage nomads who swept in from the steppes or the Asian mountains. The Scythians, the white Huns, the Seljuqs, and the Ottomans were contained for centuries at the price of Persian blood. The Indo-Europeans of the Eastern Roman Empire showed no gratitude.

They thought only of profiting from our difficulties in the East in order to gain advantage in the conflict which for thousands of years had pitted us against the principal Mediterranean power of the day.

When the Persian barrier was broken, a void was created at this meeting place of two worlds. Into this void swept Arabs from the West, then Turks and Mongols from the East. Thus, the history of eastern and western Europe, of Russia, of North Africa and of India was irrevocably altered.

As for the Sassanid Renaissance, like the European one 1,200 years later, it was a synthesis. Shapur I (A.D. 241-272) had, it is said, ordered the collection and translation of all religious, philosophical, astronomical and medical texts existing not only in the Byzantine Empire, but in India. When it is remembered that it was thanks to so-called Arab translations that Europe, from the twelfth century was to regain her knowledge of the great Greek texts, it can perhaps be claimed that there would have been no European Renaissance—or that it would have been quite different—without the work and much earlier example of the Persians, which the Arabs copied with such brilliance.

In A.D. 642 Iran suffered an Arab invasion followed by a foreign domination which should have destroyed her: the country was ruled for several centuries by the Caliphs of Baghdad. Now, as was the case with the Greeks, the conquered overcame the conquerors.

At first the Persians asserted their originality and independence by refusing Sunni doctrine and by developing the Shiite doctrine. Politically, this meant the refusal to recognize the spiritual sovereignty of the hereditary Caliphs of Baghdad; a vanquished and occupied country has nothing to call its own but its inner life.

In the political order the decisive factor in the recovery of our independence was the victorious action of an Abbasid emissary (the Abbasids were descendants of Abbas, the Prophet's uncle), Abu Muslem Khorasan. From A.D. 745-750, helped by an army with a permanent majority of Iranians, he liberated Khorasan and took possession of what is called Iraq today. Thanks to him the Abbasid dynasty succeeded that of the Umayyads in Baghdad.

The sciences and Persian art had moved eastwards to the province of Khorasan where they developed a hitherto unknown vigor and splendor. Nishapur under the Tahirids, and Samarkand and Bukhara under the Samanids became Irano-Islamic cultural centers. It was the golden age of Persian poetry, and notable poets were Ferdowsi (c. A.D. 935-1020), the prince of epic verse, and the mystics Sana'i of Ghazna and Jalal ad-din Rumi (who died in 1273). Medicine and philosophy flourished under Rhazes and Avicenna.

The breaking-up process began under the Mamelukes. The Mongol invasion merely completed the decomposition which was already well advanced, and radically destroyed the Empire. Nothing could disguise the disastrous effects of a conquest which was as brutal as it was inhumane. Genghis Khan and Hulagu destroyed most of the towns, particularly in Khorasan, and killed their populations: several million Iranians were massacred. And so the organizations which maintained Irano-Islamic cultural traditions were destroyed, and the nomadism, so much at odds with the true spirit of Persia, was intensified.

Finally, from 1383, the little that remained of urban culture was swept away by Timor Tamerlane. Historians were to cite the horrible obelisk which he had erected in Baghdad with ninety-thousand severed heads. He spared a few artisans whom he deported to Samarkand with orders to embellish it.

3

From Strength To Servitude

LEGEND MAY HAVE EXAGGERATED Tamerlane's acts of violence; it is, however, undeniable that his was a reign of terror. Persia seemed to be finally swallowed up, wiped out of history for ever. And yet the Safavid dynasty (1501–1722) witnessed a Persian renaissance.

The first Safavid, Shah Ismail (1487-1524), was to unite the country against the Uzbeks in the east and the Ottomans in the west. He sealed the moral unity of the nation when a majority rallied to Shiism, which became the official religion of the state.

Ismail was to retreat before the Portuguese under Alfonso d'Albuquerque who had taken possession of the island of Hormuz and of the neighboring coastland. It was the first time since the fall of the Roman Empire that the West had attacked Persia. It was a sign of new times, modern times: The movement which drew us towards the East had come to an end; imperceptibly the attraction towards the West had begun.

Ismail's great-grandson, Abbas the Great (1587–1629), made us powerful again, prosperous and to be dreaded. He could not regain Mesopotamia, which was lost for good in 1534 to the Ottoman Empire, but he embellished his capital, Isfahan, attracting artists and poets to it, and made of it a magnificent city of 600,000 inhabitants, "one half of the world." It was another golden age of architecture and painting.

It was Abbas, too, who authorized the Dutch and English East India companies to establish trading posts in Persia. It is true that the East India Company helped him to chase the Portuguese out of Hormuz (1622): we were not to profit from the arrangement.

From 1629 to 1736 came another century of retreats from Turkish and Russian invasions. By the agreement of 1724, these two divided our northern provinces between them, while the Afghan Ashraf occupied the whole of the east and pillaged Isfahan. Persia was dismembered and torn apart. All seemed to be lost once again.

The sad destiny of our last Safavid king the unfortunate Soltan Hoseyn, was to be miserably surrounded in his own capital by Afghan brigands. The destiny of Persia seemed sealed forever.

Nadir Shah, however, whom history has dubbed the "Persian Napoleon," was to give us back brilliance and power. Having put down the rebels in the north at Meshed and Herat, beaten Ashraf and retaken Isfahan (1729), he quickly chased away the Turks and then turned round against the Russians, who preferred not to confront him and abandoned their conquest.

Next, Nadir Shah attacked and took Kandahar and Kabul, crossed the Tsatsobi Pass—unlike the Khyber Pass, it was not defended—and came out to the rear of the enemy whom he then vanquished. Taking his prisoners with him, Nadir marched on Delhi which he entered in March 1739. Whereupon, writes an Indian historian, "the riches accumulated over 348 years changed hands in a moment." The jewels that passed according to the fortunes of war would become Persia's crown jewels, the ornament of our nation in good times and the backing of our currency in bad times. I left them in the vaults of the National Bank. God only knows what the mullahs have done with them.

On behalf of his second son, Nadir obtained the hand of Aurengzeb's granddaughter and, satisfied, he withdrew and offered Mohammad Shah his kingdom, minus the right bank of the Indus which had been part of the Achaemenid Empire.

Nadir Shah has been compared to Napoleon because of the brilliant campaigns in which he was constantly victorious. But whereas Napoleon was finally beaten by the coalition, Nadir remained invincible. However, the French Emperor was an outstanding administrator, which Nadir was not. And Napoleon sought to help his family whereas Nadir's abdominable cruelty caused him to put out his own son's eyes.

Nadir Afsharid's dynasty was succeeded by the Zand dynasty (1757–1794), which gave us Karim Khan (1757–1779) who came to be known as the "Serfs' defender." The dynasty ended in a new civil war which resulted in the coming to power of the Qajar dynasty (1794–1925).

It was then that Persia began to disintegrate into an anarchy which was all the more catastrophic for coinciding with the industrialization of the Western powers. Their expanding economic interests gave rise to Western colonialism. While the Western powers were invading the four corners of the earth—economically, militarily and politically—we lost our Caucasian provinces to the Russians by the treaties of Gulistan (1813) and Turkimanchi (1828). We also lost the province of Herat to Afghanistan, which Great Britain forced us to recognize by the Treaty of Paris, 1857, and Merv, in the northeast, to the Russians. Finally, in 1872, the province of Seistan was divided between Afghanistan and Persia.

Fath Ali Shah, the Qajar ruler who reigned from 1797 to 1834, endeavored to recapture Georgia. He greatly admired Napoleon and he warmly welcomed the "Comte de Gardanne" and the military-diplomatic mission which the French emperor sent to Teheran in 1807. This mission studied and explored the Persian roads with a view to sending a powerful French expedition into India.

In Egypt, Napoleon had carefully studied Nadir Shah's victorious campaign of 1739. Today his plan is seen as a mere dream. But the recorded correspondence of Fath Ali Shah, his son Abbas Mirza, and General Gardanne with Napoleon and Champagny, the French foreign minister, reveals the emperor's real intentions. He saw Persia both as the natural bastion of the West and its passageway to the East. He consequently felt "this strategic area of primary importance" should be put to use for offensive and defensive purposes. It was first a matter of containing the Russians: The Persians could be counted on "provided they had twenty thousand guns and a good artillery at their disposition."

Next it was necessary to train seriously and to make use of "the 144,000-strong Persian cavalry, troops of the first order" as the vanguard of the French expedition to India: "An expedition," wrote Gardanne on January 26, 1808, "which everyone in Teheran is thinking about."

The French headquarters in Teheran, Isfahan and Shiraz, calculated that "the Indus campaign" would last from five to seven months depending on whether the Grande Armée advanced by road (through Aleppo,

Baghdad, Basra, Shiraz, and Yazd) or arrived by the Black Sea and Trebizond. One part of the army would then advance through Erzurum, Hamadan, Yazd, and Herat, and the other through Tauros, Teheran, the Khorasan.

Gardanne added: "A beast of burden will be needed for every two men. . . . cannons, cannonballs, and gunpowder will be manufactured on the spot: Persia has a very fine quality of saltpeter. . . . the Indus sikhs at war with the English can muster 50,000 cavalry."

Unfortunately, Fath Ali gained nothing that he wanted from the French alliance. The Russian troops overran Northern Persia and Gardanne wrote to Napoleon: "An English mission is coming up the Persian Gulf, led by Sir Harford Jones who is a great blackguard and laden with gold."

At the time the emperor was in Spain chasing the British expedition with the intention of putting his brother, Joseph, on the abandoned Spanish throne. His plan for an expedition to India by way of Persia was dropped as a result of his armies having to fight on the Danube in 1809 and, three years later, on the Moskva.

4

The Road to India and Oil

UNDER FATH ALI S SUCCESSORS (Mohammad, 1834-1848; Nasiri ed-Din Shah, 1848-1896; and Mozaffar ed-Din, 1896-1907); Persian weakness turned to apathy. Although at the outset of Mohammad Shah's reign we were still fighting for the province of Herat which belongs to us, we were destined to abandon it finally and to recognize the kingdom of Afghanistan merely as the result of a British threat. And why did "Her Majesty's Government consider the occupation [*sic*] of the province of Herat to be an act of hostility?" Not because we, the Iranians, represented a threat to India, but certainly because Russian consuls would have opened offices in a reconquered Herat.

From the Treaty of Paris in 1857 until 1921, our unfortunate country had no government which dared to move one soldier, grant one concession, or pass one law concerning Iranians without the agreement, tacit or otherwise, of either the British ambassador or the Russian ambassador, or of both. Our policies—if such they can be called—were developed in the two embassies, and two governments barely disguised the fact that they considered Persia to be a sort of "untouchable" servant. Their diplomatic communications were orders, which we carried out, and in the event of our showing any sign of recalcitrance, they became threats. As a stopgap, Great Britain would "invade" us: An "expeditionary force" (several hundred men) would land in the Gulf. Everything would be returned to order except when tribes like the Tchahontahi or the Tangestani of their own accord exterminated the expeditionary force. At all costs the English had to keep the road to India open.

It was along this route that two French scientists, the geologist Cotte and the archeologist Jacques de Morgan, found evidence of deposits of petroleum. In Persia since antiquity it had been known as "Napht" and used by Zoroastrians for their sacred fires. It had long been known that the Persian subsoil, especially in the southeastern part of the country, was rich in oil. In 1872 an English baron, Julius von Reuter, obtained wide-ranging commercial concessions. His efforts to profit from them were in vain and he gave them up before losing his entire fortune. Happily, he took consolation in the creation of a press agency that is still well-known today.

Success came more readily a few years later to the two Frenchmen. It was easier for them to find a financier who was interested in their discovery. The British minister in Persia, Sir Henry Drummond, put them in touch with the Australian banker, William Knox d'Arcy, who lived in London.

Knox d'Arcy had a massive fortune which came from a gold mine in Queensland, Australia. A taste for adventure combined with a sound business sense persuaded him that he could double his money with black gold. On May 28, 1901, after lengthy negotiations which had been complicated by the somewhat menacing demands of the Russians, the Shah finally granted Knox d'Arcy an exclusive sixty-year concession "to find, extract, transport and commercialize natural gas, petroleum, asphalt and other derivatives of petroleum throughout the land"—with the exception of the provinces bordering on Tsarist Russia. In fact, on this occasion, Knox d'Arcy had been excessively optimistic. The sums which had to be invested were soon beyond his purse and he had to hand over the concession to the Anglo-Persian Oil company.

It was not until May 26, 1908, that oil finally flowed at Masjid-i-Suleiman (or Suleiman's Mosque from its proximity to the ruins of the temple). Knox d'Arcy's name was destined from that time to take its place in the history of petroleum, although he never set foot in Persia and probably never saw a barrel of oil in his life.

Meanwhile, on August 31, 1907, Great Britain and Russia had signed a decree which divided Persia between them.

From 1905, the Russian revolutionary agitation, with its uprisings at Tiflis and Baku, had provoked a politico-religious movement in Teheran. The movement, which was favored by Great Britain, obligated the weak Mozzaffar ed-Din Shah to grant a paper constitution in 1906, only a few days before his death. But, apart from the election of an assembly—the election was completely dominated by feudal landowners—there were few real reforms.

The social and political climate in Persia was a nightmare. The central government was so weak that its authority did not even extend to the whole of the capital, and the army and the police force were almost nonexistent. The few soldiers were badly paid or not paid at all and thus were obligated to take on small jobs in order to survive. In addition, they took orders from Russian officers in the North and English officers in the South.

Strength alone ruled. This was in the hands of large landowners and the heads of local tribes who, under British control, were entrusted with the security of oil-producing operations. In the countryside it was in the hands of brigands, and thieves in the towns.

Persia was one of the poorest countries in the world. The government had to borrow from merchants in order to entertain a foreign guest. The only individuals to prosper were engaged in trading abroad. Foreigners had been granted the right to exploit the principal national resources and services: oil, fishing, telegraphy, customs, etc. Agriculture, craft, and commerce remained in the Middle Ages. Serfdom still existed.

Health conditions were appalling. Not only was the average life expectancy a mere thirty years, but the infant mortality rate was one of the highest in the world. Malnutrition and unhygienic conditions afflicted a people who had been a model of health and vitality. The total absence of hygiene caused typhoid, malaria, and trachoma to become endemic in some regions, while epidemics of the plague and cholera were not unusual, nor were famines caused by drought. Sadly, thanks to today's so-called government, cholera again plagues my country.

Ignorance walked hand in hand with poverty and sickness. Fewer than one percent of the population were literate. There was only one lycée in

Teheran. Women did not go to school and were deprived of all rights. All the privileges of Western material civilization which, to a certain extent, reached the Ottoman Empire, India, and our other neighbors, were practically unknown in Iran. There were no railways, no proper roads, no cars, no electricity, no telephones. Where any of these were to be found, they were considered a real luxury. Material and spiritual poverty marched side by side with the spread of corruption, deceit, hypocrisy, opium addiction, and superstition.

This decadence may have resulted partly from the weakness and ignorance of the Iranian people, but it sprang, above all, from the impotence of the Persian authorities, from the egoism of the feudal aristocracy and from the deliberate will of foreign colonialists. Many of the British remembered Nadir and dreaded the Iranians. Also, they were putting into practice a policy of a no-man's-land between Russia and India. Like a condemned man who has lost all hope, the dying country awaited a *coup de grâce*; and it little mattered whether it came from the north or the south. It was at this moment that a man of strength came forward: My father.

5

My Father

WHEN BRITAIN AND RUSSIA signed the 1907 treaty dividing Iran between them, my father was nearly thirty. He was a giant of a man, loved by the soldiers who served under him in a brigade of Iranian Cossacks, and feared by the brigand leaders who terrorized the countryside and were in the pay of large landholders. My father was the stuff of legends and there were legends of him aplenty.

By World War I he had a national reputation and the nickname of Reza Maxim, a tribute to his prowess with the early machine gun at a time when there couldn't have been more than five or six such guns in the country. One contemporary photograph shows him standing behind his Maxim gun, just after enemy bullets had smashed the weapon. But neither Maxim gun nor reputation enabled my father to do more than watch with anguish as Persia became in 1915 a battleground between Germans and Turks on the one hand and Britons and Russians on the other. Our people became bystanders to their own history.

The situation grew worse after the Anglo-Iranian treaty of 1919 which in effect made Iran a British protectorate. Meanwhile, the Bolshevik revolution rumbled on in the northern provinces and proclamation of a Soviet republic seemed imminent.

During that time, my father and his Cossacks lived in the fields trying to preserve what fragmented order remained. There wasn't much. It was a time to despair of the nation. The central government was paralyzed while bandit leaders carved up the country. Then, as now, Iran had no law, no order, no army, no police. Ignorant and self-interested clergy dispensed what justice there was, "sharing" that task with bandits whose courts meted out swift and terrible punishment. Foreigners, however, even if recognized criminals, were immune from prosecution thanks to the post-war treaties imposed on Persia. No one went out at night, not even in Teheran, except for dire medical emergencies and then as often as not a doctor could not be found. People were robbed or murdered on street corners.

Communications had all but collapsed. Travelers from Teheran, fearful of highway bandits, went through Russia in order to reach Meshed in the northeast. Those who had business in the province of Khuzestan to the southwest went by way of Turkey and Mesopotamia.

At one point, the visible decay of our nation had so filled my father with disgust and despair that he deliberately exposed himself to enemy fire. While up north with his soldiers fighting yet another gang of bandits, he swung onto his white horse and galloped toward enemy lines. Frightened at first by the sudden apparition of this giant on his white steed, the bandits were too stunned to react. Then, when they opened fire, they shot at random without taking careful aim. As a result, my father was able to spur his horse through the barrage unharmed.

Perhaps it was an omen. For, shortly after my father's return to Teheran from a victorious campaign in the north, my twin sister Ashraf and I were born on October 26, 1919. Death having rejected him and glad for a son and heir, Reza Khan decided to live and to fight on. First he engineered the dismissal of the Russian officers, who were only nominally all "White Russian." Next, he took the Iranian Cossacks in hand and in August 1920 found himself in command of a force of 2,500. By that time the situation in Iran had changed from bad to worse. Reza Khan realized that it was a question of survival for his country and decided to act.

With the support of liberal and democratic groups, early in 1921 he left his headquarters at Ghazvin with 1,200 horsemen and marched on Teheran. His Cossacks surrounded the capital and on February 21, 1921, Reza Khan forced the ruler, Ahmad Shah, to appoint a new government. The coup was carried out with such dispatch and so few casualties that the commander of British forces in Persia, General Ironside, is said to have told friends that "Reza Khan is the only man capable of saving Iran."

One of my father's allies was a young political journalist named Seyed Zia ed-Din Taba Taba'i, a revolutionary who was well equipped to bring political pressure to bear in the capital while my father applied military force. Zia ed-Din became Prime Minister, while my father became Minister of War. However, Zia ed-Din, instinctively the radical reformer, was unable to execute any of his plans. This together with his increasingly pro-British leanings, forced him, after only three months, to resign his post and leave the country. Seyed, incidentally, stayed away until my father was exiled in 1941. Then he returned to form an opposition political party, Erade-Ye Melli (National Will), a fact that did not prevent us from becoming friends later on.

With Zia ed-Din gone, my father persuaded Ahmad Shah to form a new government in which my father retained the War Ministry. The government was no sooner in office than Ahmad Shah left for an extended stay in Europe. In 1923 Reza became a Prime Minister in order to more effectively unite our bitterly divided country. He had no intention then of dethroning the king. On the contrary, he repeatedly asked him to return and when he finally agreed, my father met him at Bandar-Bushehr on the Persian Gulf. But Ahmad Shah was weak and uninterested and eager to return to Europe. When he finally left again for France—where he eventually died—my father realized that halfway measures no longer sufficed. The absence of a strong, effective head of state had proved intolerable.

Reza Khan had been greatly influenced by the reforms Kemal Ataturk had introduced in Turkey and for a time he hoped to emulate his neighbor's achievements and turn Iran into a modern republic. But those efforts ran into great opposition from the clergy, politicians, and merchants because Persia, unlike Turkey, was an empire in which only the crown united diverse ethnic groups with their different languages and cultures: Kurds, Arabs, Azerbaijanis, Baluchistanis and others. Accordingly, on October 31, 1925, our parliament voted the Qajar dynasty out of power. Election of a constituent assembly followed and with only four nay votes, it handed the 2,500-year old Persian crown to generallissimo Reza Khan.

The crown allowed him to push with greater vigor the reforms he had begun soon after the 1921 coup. Just how successfully he did so, and how much admiration his efforts garnered from the man he had sought to emulate, Ataturk, came some years after his coronation when he went on a state visit to Turkey and the honor guard's standard bearer knelt before him. A first step after the coup had been conclusion of a friendship and non-aggression pact with the Soviet Union, which voided the privileges and conditions of earlier agreements. At the same time the Anglo-Iranian treaty of 1919, never approved by parliament, was denounced. Both moves reduced foreign power and influence over Iranian government action.

Equally important was the re-establishment of domestic unity and the removal of foreign interference in Iran's internal affairs. The British, to cite one example, had sold shares in the Anglo-Persian oil company to some tribal chieftains, who in exchange agreed to maintain law and order in the oil-producing regions. The opportunity for British manipulation was obvious. My father solved that problem simply enough: he bought up all the outstanding shares and subjugated one tribe after the other in the center, south and southwest of the country.

But creation of a strong army ranked first on his list of priorities. After his march on Teheran he complained, "if only I had a thousand guns of the same caliber" and he meant rifles, not field pieces. Without adequate armed strength, he knew enduring national unity could not be achieved. In the twenties he expanded our armed forces to one division, an autonomous brigade and special highway patrols. In addition, he built small forts along strategic highway crossroads. Safe passage within a country is a basic prerequisite of national unity. Next, he built a navy and an air force. Officers were imported from France and Iranian cadets sent to St. Cyr, Saumur and Saint-Maixent for officer training. Later on, I would be instructed by St. Cyr-trained officers.

A rapid program of industrialization was launched to begin domestic production of basic manufactured goods. Agricultural reform was on his mind but something he never had time to implement. That was left to me and the White Revolution I began in the 1960s.

The stranglehold of foreign monopolies on the economic and social life of the country was gradually broken, though it was no easy task. Belgium ran the customs services with the entire revenue used to pay off our external debts. The Swedes ran the police force; our banks were in the hands of Russians, Britons and Turks. The British printed and issued our currency and owned the telegraph system. My father moved boldly to give Persia its own money. He issued new banknotes backed by gold and the crown jewels, whose most brilliant stones date back to Nadir Shah's triumph in India.

The British Crown owns the Koh-i-Noor diamond, the Mountain of Light, but we have the Daria-i-Noor or Sea of Light, perhaps an even more beautiful stone. Along with the other crown jewels this magnificent diamond is kept in the vaults of the Central Bank. Other coffers in the vaults are filled with pearls and diamonds. Our dynasty never stopped enriching this treasure with gifts and purchases of precious stones. And we have always considered this the property of the nation and the people, a point worth making today when Reza Shah's achievements are being deliberately eradicated from Iranian consciousness.

What did the 15- and 16-year-old rioters know of my father when they knocked down his statues in our towns and cities after my ouster? The fact that he had pulled our country up from nothing—that he had built towns, schools, the first university, hospitals, factories, roads, ports and the first power station—seems to have been lost on these so-called revolutionaries. And, he began doing all these things before issuing his own currency, a sign of his grit and determination. Both qualities came to the fore again, when in 1927 he began construction of the Trans-Iranian railroad to link the Caspian Sea with the Persian Gulf. The thousand mile line was completed in 1938. He defied the international oil powers for the first time in 1932 by cancelling the Anglo-Iranian oil concessions, originally granted to d'Arcy in 1901, and then concluding a new deal with the British. When he took power in 1921, Iranian oil production was only 2.3 million tons. By 1938 output had risen to 10.3 million tons (later dwarfed by the 300 million tons Iran produced in 1977.)

My father's coronation took place on April 25, 1926, and as the new emperor, he became Reza Shah Pahlavi. The name Pahlavi has deep roots in our country's history: it is the name of the official language and writings of the emperors during the Sassanid era. It is the patronym which he left me and which I bequeath to my children. During the ceremony I was proclaimed Prince and Heir Apparent. I was only seven years old.

My father loved us dearly and deeply. There were eleven of us, all told, some my half-brothers and sisters. Our love for him was full of admiration though we held him in respectful awe. Broad-shouldered and tall, he had prominent and rugged features, but it was his piercing eyes that arrested anybody who met him. Those eyes could make a strong man shrivel up inside. Eventually I was able to say to him what needed saying without fear of contradiction or censure. But that took a long time. He was a powerful and formidable man and the good heart that beat beneath his rough cavalryman's exterior was not easily reached. Yet even his enemies realized that he was one of those men sent by Providence through the centuries to keep a nation from slipping into oblivion.

He was impetuous and determined, qualities he needed to overcome the terrible difficulties that marked his reign. He grew up illiterate and had to teach himself how to read. As a grown man he felt no shame in starting from the beginning. Each day at the end of his army duties, he would sit patiently at his studies in his barracks, learning to read and write with the help of one of his friends. He prepared his lessons by the dim lamps, and when he was tired, he would come out of his tiny room and stand gazing at the twinkling lights of Teheran in the distance. He literally pulled himself up by his own bootstraps, and his country with him. As a ruler, he was out with his people all the time. He inspected everything, not just the armed forces. Sometimes I thought he supervised every stone put atop another. He did not surround himself with the trappings of oriental monarchs. Instead, he saw his imperial duties as a kind of military service.

He slept on a simple mattress on the floor and was up at five each morning. By 7:30 he had finished reading through daily reports and began receiving people. As a young man I would go to his study at around eleven each morning and talk to him for half an hour or so about the problems of the country or anything else that interested him or me. Then around 11:30 we would sit down to a family lunch. After lunch my father rested and at about 2 P.M. started his afternoon work. It consisted chiefly of inspecting the army and new civil projects and institutions. The Council of Ministers, as our Cabinet is called, often held afternoon meetings in his presence. Then from 6 to 8 P.M., after all his other work, he would study the reports he had received during the day. Exactly at 8 P.M. he took his supper, and he retired at 10 P.M. However, he used to say that even in bed his plans were revolving and forming in his mind; thus he was never idle.

Apart from relaxation with his family, my father almost never devoted any time to recreation. Perhaps once or twice a year he would go hunting for two or three hours. Mainly he got his exercise through walking. In my memory it seems as if he were *always* walking, either pacing up and down in his office or inspecting troops or projects on foot or, in the late afternoon, taking long walks in his garden. Often he would hold audiences while walking; those whom he received were on such occasions expected to pace up and down with him. And whenever Reza Shah was walking, he was also thinking.

His labors were not limited to industrial and military modernization of our country for he was equally interested in social reforms. Thus in 1926-27 he introduced a judiciary system modelled on that of France. He mandated compulsory, lay primary education even though we lacked competent teachers. And in the process he suppressed the often inquisitional legal powers of the clergy.

It is essential to understand the fundamental importance of this evolution which, moreover, occurred throughout the Islamic Near East. The institution by my father, and the development by myself, of a modern political regime, partly inspired by the West, have deprived the clergy of a large part of their erstwhile privileges.

Some of the Shiite priests at first fell back on the ancient political position concerning the very nature of power: all temporal power whatsoever must be usurped. Instead they should have taken advantage of the situation to develop their spiritual life, thereby increasing and spreading their moral and civilizing influence.

But it must be acknowledged that, had my father not curtailed political efforts of certain clerics, the task which he had undertaken would have been far more difficult. It would have been a long time before Iran became a modern state. Because my father had little respect for certain particularly fanatical and sectarian hierarchies, he was said, quite wrongly, to be irreligious. He was a deeply sincere believer, as I am myself. His faith was that of a courageous and honest man.

The spiritual authority of the clergy remained incontestable and uncontested. The moral primacy of the spiritual over the temporal being indisputable and undisputed, it was a matter of bringing Iran into the twentieth century, whereas today's efforts are towards turning the clock back. Reza Shah asserted that in the twentieth century it was impossible for a nation to survive in obscurantism. True spirituality should exist *over and above* politics and economics. Reza Shah was too sincere a believer to see God as a sort of superior electoral agent or chief engineer of the oil wells.

He named all his sons after the Imam Reza—with a first name by which they were distinguished—because he had a particular veneration for this descendant of our sainted Ali. Reza Shah frequently went on a pilgrimage to the shrine of Imam Reza at Meshed. Imam Reza's Foundation was abandoned and in debt when Reza Shah came to power. Reza Shah restored it which was no easy task. Created as a religious institution, it had in better times been the recipient of land and monies bequeathed the foundation for religious purposes or charity. Usually the ruling king would be custodian or director of that foundation, but a succession of weak rulers had left Imam Reza in as desolate a state as the rest of the country. My father put things to right and set the foundation on a new path to growth. (It is worth noting, perhaps, that the Imam Reza Foundation has nothing to do with the Pahlavi Foundation, which my family and I founded much later.)

During my reign, the Imam Reza Foundation became one of the most important and most prosperous in all Islam. Gifts from the faithful, among them myself, have turned this foundation into an extraordinary religious complex, owning factories, mechanized agricultural co-operatives, hospitals and numerous charitable organizations. Let me say, in passing, that I also restored and enriched many monuments and mosques both in Iran and abroad. It is well known that donations to foundations are non-recuperable. Now the self-styled new government in Teheran has confiscated them.

My father also took care to protect our religion against the propaganda of an intolerant materialism which demanded that the "mosques be razed." But this did not mean that he accepted all the claims of men of religion who lived obstinately behind the times.

He decided, then, that the citizens should finally abandon oriental dress—their wide trousers, turbans and bonnets. Some people did not agree with this. And when women were asked to give up their black veil, measures "taken in the simple name of good sense" were actively contested by part of the clergy. I was to be far less intransigent. During my reign, women and girls were perfectly free to wear, or not to wear, the *chaddor.*

My father's reforms had reduced the clergy's authority in secular matters. Thus, from 1926 a certain section of the ecclesiastical hierarchy was openly opposed to the Shah's reforms and to Iran's metamorphosis into a modern nation. This opposition made itself felt again at the time of the 1952-53 uprising, in 1963 and in 1978-79.

It was thanks to my father's example that, at an early age, I was able to understand the power of prayer, which was never a mere recitation of formulas learned by heart.

Numerous chroniclers have published more or less accurate accounts of my childhood. Shortly after my father's coronation, I fell ill with typhoid fever, and for weeks I hovered between life and death. The worst was feared, until one night, in a dream, I saw Ali, who in our faith was the chief lieutenant of Mohammed (much as, according to Christian doctrine, St. Peter was a leading disciple of Jesus Christ).

In my dream, Ali had with him his famous two-pronged sword, which is often seen in paintings of him. He was sitting on his heels on the floor, and in his hands he held a bowl containing a liquid. He told me to drink, which I did. The next day, the crisis of my fever was over, and I was on the road to recovery.

A little later, during the summer, on my way to Emamzadeh-Daoud, a place of pilgrimage in the mountains, I fell from my horse on to rocks and passed out. I was taken for dead but I had not so much as a scratch. In falling I had a vision of one of our saints, Abbas, who cradled me as I fell.

This dream and this vision were followed some time later by an apparition near the Shimran Royal Palace. It was Imam, the descendant of the Prophet who, according to our faith, must reappear on earth to save the world. Dream, vision, apparition: some of my Western readers may dismiss it as an illusion, or put forward some psychological explanation. But remember that a faith in non-material things has always been characteristic of peoples of the East. I have found that this is also true of many Westerners.

Long after I had emerged from childhood fantasies (if any among my readers feel more comfortable to call them that), there occurred four other incidents which may help explain why my childhood faith has continued strong within me.

The first was an airplane accident in 1948. I was flying a Tiger Moth near Isfahan, where work was being carried out on an irrigation dam. The general commanding the Isfahan division, a cavalry officer, was with me. Suddenly, in mid-flight, my engine went dead. We had to make a forced landing in a mountainous region in a ravine full of rocks and boulders.

As every pilot knows, a plane has a stalling speed below which it will go into a spin. With the engine gone I had no throttle, nor could I maneuver within the narrow confines of the ravine; the only thing was to maintain my speed by going down then and there. Just before we struck, I pulled on the stick to raise the plane's nose and avert a head-on collision with a barrier of rock lying directly in front of us. The plane had barely enough speed left to clear the barrier, and could not surmount a big stone lying just beyond. When we collided with it the undercarriage was completely torn off, but at least that helped to reduce our speed. The plane started to slide on its belly over the rock-strewn ground. A moment later the propeller hit a large boulder, and the plant turned a slow and deliberate somersault, coming to a halt with the fuselage upside down. There we were, hanging by our seat belts in the open cockpit. Neither of us had suffered so much as a scratch. I remember that the scene amused me so much that I burst out laughing, but my upside-down companion didn't think it was funny.

Another airplane had been following us. It landed behind the village. Meanwhile some people in our party who were to meet us had reached us by car. They were somewhat concerned. I hastened to reassure them, and said: "Well, now I am going on in the other airplane!" I was surrounded by generals who protested vigorously. Seeing that I had no intention of giving in, they lay down in front of the aircraft: "No, sir you cannot leave!"

So I finished my journey by car and I had the satisfaction of arriving in Isfahan in time for what I had to do.

On another occasion, a similar accident befell me. I was at the controls when we entered a very narrow defile. I immediately realized that it would be quite impossible for us to cross the mountain pass. I was obliged to make a half turn just as the dials showed that we were losing speed and managed, with the wings vertical and the ground only a few meters away, to right my airplane, thus, against all expectations, defying the laws of gravity and of aerodynamics. In this desperate maneuver a certain death awaited us. Logically we should have crashed.

The young pilot who was with me was so surprised to find us both still alive on landing that he wanted, there and then, to give me a demonstration of his own talents. I realized that he was eager not to be outclassed. He wanted to loop the loop, to skim upside down over the land and to right the aircraft before completing his aerobatics.

Since I knew that he was perfectly capable of performing such a difficult feat of flying, I accepted. Having flown nose down, he unfortunately did not succeed in righting the plane, and crashed before my eyes. Such great cruelty of fate once again forced me to conclude that my hour had not yet come.

The attempt on my life on February 4, 1949, convinced me once more that I was protected. That day, in the early afternoon, I was to attend the annual ceremony to commemorate the founding of Teheran University. I was dressed in uniform and was going to preside over the presentation of diplomas.

I took my place at the head of the official procession just after 3 P.M. Photographers had lined up to take pictures when a man broke away from the group and rushed at me. Not ten feet away from me he pulled a gun and fired at point-blank range. Three bullets whizzed through my hat and knocked it off but did not burn a hair. A fourth bullet went through my cheek and came out under my nose without doing much damage. He fired a fifth time and I knew instinctively that the shot was aimed at my heart. In a fraction of a second, I moved slightly and the bullet hit my shoulder. One bullet remained. Then the assassin's gun jammed. Despite the blood dripping from my face, my enemies would say afterwards that he had used cotton bullets.

Unfortunately my assailant, a certain Fakhr Arai, was killed immediately. Perhaps it was in someone's interest that he not be questioned. What little we discovered about him was strange enough to motivate efforts to silence him. Arai was involved with an ultraconservative religious group that was comprised of the most backward religious fanatics. We also found Communist literature and brochures in his home relating to the Tudeh, the Iranian Communist party. Significantly or not, the Tudeh happened to be holding its national congress at the time of the attempted assassination. And there was a third connection: Arai's mistress was the daughter of the British embassy's gardener.

The British had their fingers in strange pies. They were always interested in forging links with diverse groups in nations they wished to control, and they had long exercised a good deal of control over Iran. There is little doubt that London was involved with the Tudeh in various ways and of course the British had ties to the most reactionary clergy in the country. All this happened thirty years ago, yet I cannot help but wonder if in the person of Fakhr Arai I had seen the first glimmer of what would later come to be known as "Islamic Marxism." Of course the two concepts are irreconcilable—unless those who profess Islam do not understand their own religion or pervert it for their own political ends. Arai does not seem to have been a clever man and might have confused the two opposing dogmas, aided in that confusion perhaps by subtle British propaganda to which he may have been exposed in the embassy.

As I say, all this is conjecture, but persuasive conjecture for me. The roots of my downfall grew deep and in many places. By 1949 I had announced plans to revise the constitution so the king would have the power to dissolve parliament. That would have destroyed the parliamentary oligarchy then ruling Iran and sharply increased royal power, the last thing Britain wanted. Her policy needed a malleable king.

The fourth incident occurred many years later when a soldier armed with a machine gun broke into the Marble Palace on April 10, 1965. I was working in my study on the first floor at the time the shooting started. I thought that maybe a thousand rifles were attacking the house, because of the echo of that machine gun in the hall. Since I had no arms in my study in those days, I just stood there, not knowing what to do. One bullet came right through the door of my study barely missing me. Suddenly, the shooting stopped. When I opened the door, I saw two of my civilian guards and the would-be assassin dead on the floor. A gardener and a valet had also been wounded in the fracas. Upon investigation of this assassination attempt, it was learned that two intellectuals and this soldier were behind the plot. The intellectuals were pardoned. As a result, one of them became a loyal supporter of mine, who later was gainfully employed in the television division of my government. It is sad to say that in 1979 he was executed by Mr. Khomeini.

The miraculous failure of these assassination attempts once again proved to me that my life was protected. I have always had the feeling that only "that which is written" can come to pass.

My faith has always dictated my behavior as a man and as a head of state, and I believe that I have never ceased to be the defender of our faith. An atheist civilization is not truly civilized and I have always taken care that the White Revolution to which I have dedicated so many years of my reign should, on all points, conform to the principles of Islam.

I believe that the essence of Islam is justice, and that I followed the holy Koran when I decreed and organized a national, communal solidarity, when our White Revolution abolished privilege and redistributed wealth and income more equitably.

For me, religious beliefs are the heart and soul of the spiritual life of all communities. Without this, all societies, however materially advanced, go astray. True faith is the best guarantee of moral health and spiritual strength. It represents for all men a superior protection against life's vicissitudes; and for every nation it constitutes the most powerful spiritual guardian.

Our people had an opportunity to live under the banner of the most progressive religious principles possible: I am referring to the sacred principles of Islam, which at each stage of individual or societal progress marks the forward path. All those who participated in our Revolution and believed in it could justly take pride in the fact that it was inspired by the basic spirit of Islam.

My desire to make the roots of this spirit penetrate ever more into the soul of our people was not accompanied by any animosity towards other religions. On the contrary, history will one day show that one of the characteristics of my reign was tolerance. Iran since the time of Cyrus has always been a land of refuge—except during periods of trouble when the central authority had collapsed before factions. Such is the case today.

We had the greatest respect for all those who, living in our country, professed other faiths, for they were a part of Iranian society and also because all faith imposes respect upon the beholder.

6

"Young Man"

WHEN I WAS SIX years old I was entrusted to the care of a French governess, Madame Arfa, who had married an Iranian. To her, I owe my ability to speak and read French as if it were my own language, as well as my interest in Western culture. I was also exposed to her violent hatred of all things German and listened to many tirades against the despised "boches."

Under her tutelage I began dreaming dreams unusual for a boy my age. But then I already knew that I would not lead the life of an ordinary boy. Thus, I dreamed of making my country's peasants happy and having every man judged by just laws. These were dreams that never left me and which to a large degree I managed to realize in later life.

Though my father had done much to improve Iran's educational system, much still needed to be done. As a result many Iranian children from good families in those days were educated abroad. So, after graduation from the elementary military school in Teheran in May 1931, my brother, Ali Reza, and I were sent abroad to obtain the kind of top-notch schooling Reza Shah wanted for us. In 1931, we embarked at Bandar Pahlavi, a small port on the Caspian Sea, on our way to Baku in Russia. From there we took a train across the Soviet Union and Europe to Lausanne. It was an enormous trip for anyone in those days, and even more dramatic for young boys.

My father sent several other boys with us to make sure we would not lose contact with our people. Among them was a boy named Hossein Fardoust. I had known him at court since we were both six years old; he was to become one of my closest friends and advisors and ultimately betray me. He is now head of Savama, Khomeini's Secret Service. Mehrpour Teymourtach, the son of my father's court minister was also with me. Later his father fell out of favor and my friend left school.

We spent our first year in Switzerland at the École Nouvelle in Lausanne, and then moved on to LeRosey, an elite Swiss school that has educated the sons of the world's best families. Not surprisingly, given my early childhood training with Madame Arfa, I was able to adjust easily to Swiss life. I was well read for my age and my ability to handle the French language was up to Le Rosey's standards. By and large the next four years were happy and productive. I followed the scientific course, not Latin and Greek, and did well in most subjects. My favorites were history, geography, and science, though geometry was not a strong point with me. I was petrified every time the mathematics professor entered the classroom, as were most other boys. Yet looking back, I remember him as a very nice man. His wife was a writer and she was very sweet to me.

My social life was varied enough, though I preferred the friendship of older boys. My popularity with the others was bolstered by a large supply of pistachio nuts which I kept in my room. Finally, for my last two years my younger brothers joined me at Le Rosey.

Intellectually, my education confirmed my passion for history and for the great men who had important roles in shaping it. I admired the emperor Charles V, for example, for his military genius in establishing what was then the best infantry in Europe and for giving such prestige and strength to Spain. Peter the Great unified Russia and I found his accomplishments fascinating, though I was concerned about the human costs of his achievements. And Catherine the Great continued the course he had set. The French, of course, were closest to my thinking. I admired the great French rulers like Henri IV and Louis XIV, the Sun King, and most of all Napoleon, a truly extraordinary leader. And, with great reservation, I studied the history ot the French cardinals who had advised and directed their kings. I never thought the Peacock Throne could stand a Richelieu or a Mazarin. I shudder to think of my reign with clerical advisors, especially in light of the results of today's so-called Islamic Republic.

In 1936, at the age of 17, I returned home to Iran for the first time in five years. It was like visiting a different country. I recognized nothing. The sleepy port city of Pahlavi had become a modern Western town. My father had razed Teheran's old walls. Streets were paved and asphalted. The city had begun to take on the look and style of a European capital. I saw it all at first as if in a dream. My father met me and we drove in an open car through the streets of the city. Thousands of young people lined our route, tossing flowers. One full bouquet hit me in the face and my father similarly received another. The welcome was overwhelming, and surely one of the most moving experiences of my life. I had little time, however, to savor the reception or to think deeply about the new Iran growing up around me. My father sent me to our military school where I studied under Iranian and French officers trained at St. Cyr.

In the spring of 1938 I graduated as a second lieutenant and immediately took up my duties as an army inspector. My relationship with my father grew closer. I spent several hours a day with him and learned much about his vision of rule and about the practicalities of being a king. Soon I was the only man in the kingdom able to express my opinions to him even when they contradicted his own. We often debated land reform. My ideas had not yet crystallized but I knew that the lot of our peasants had to be improved and improved from the top. At the time I had a plan for a debt moratorium that would free farmers from payments to their landlords for several years and let them use the money instead to build houses and buy cattle. Eventually I wanted them to own their own land. I was troubled by the vast land tracts my father purchased. One day we discussed the issue and he explained that he concentrated his land-buying along our country's frontier primarily for national security reasons. Although he had in mind a better life for the peasants, he knew it would take time and that national security had to come first.

My father took me on his frequent inspection trips through the country. He wanted me to know the land and how to rule it. I studied his role as military leader and especially remember his vivid descriptions of the chaotic situation of our country during the terrible years from 1915 to 1921. He had an uncanny understanding of international politics and its implications for Iran. In the late thirties he sensed the advent of war. He worried that it would begin before Iran's armies were capable of defending our neutrality against all comers. His worst fears were realized. World War II broke out on September 1, 1939, long before we were ready to mount an effective defense.

Much has been made of my father's alleged admiration for Hitler and for the Germans. Certainly Britain and Russia used his supposed links to the Third Reich as a pretext for invading our country in 1941 and they are still cited in their history books as fact. This was not fact but myth. My father mistrusted Hitler from the very beginning, if for no other reason than as an authoritarian ruler he was deeply suspicious of another who used such brutal methods of rule. And he had learned from recent history: On his state visit to Turkey in the late twenties, he had listened intently to his hosts' graphic description of life under the German boot during Turkey's World War I alliance with the Kaiser when Berlin dominated Turkish life and the Germans treated the Turks like dirt. He had been deeply impressed then and now was deeply suspicious of German intent. True, we employed a number of German technicians, but their employment had nothing to do with politics. They were quite simply excellent at their jobs and vital to our modernization drive—as they would be again in the sixties and seventies when German technological expertise was utilized to implement my own White Revolution. In any event, when war came my father declared Iran neutral and hoped for the best.

During the early years of World War II, it seemed as if we might be spared. That hope began to fade after the Axis powers invaded the Balkans in April 1941 and German soldiers stood distressingly close on the Bulgarian border. The Nazi invasion of Russia on June 22, 1941, filled us with new foreboding. My father promptly reiterated Iran's neutrality in forceful language.

But once again history and geography conspired against us. Hitler's Blitzkrieg in the East threatened to bring Russia to her knees in a matter of months. It was clear the Soviets could not survive the German onslaughts without Allied support. Shipping supplies through Murmansk in the far north, although possible, was difficult and slow. Sending supplies through the Mediterranean that summer was out of the question, since the Axis dominated the air and British ships could barely reach Egypt. Turkey would not allow passage through the Dardanelles, even assuming supply ships eluded German bases in Greece. And once in the Black Sea, Berlin controlled the coasts of Bulgaria and Romania. The only safe and relatively rapid supply passage was through the Persian Gulf. Thus, Iran became an area of prime strategic and tactical importance.

By July 1941, our neutral position had grown precarious. The first warnings came from my brother-in-law, Egypt's King Farouk, whose sister Fawzia was my wife. Farouk told his father-in-law, then ambassador in Teheran, to warn me that recent British troop movements might be directed at Iran. In turn, I alerted my father. Reza Shah immediately cabled his minister in London, Mr. Moghadam, and instructed him to determine Britain's real intention. Unfortunately, we received no reply. The Churchill government was not interested in seeking our permission to ship supplies across Iran. Moreover, the Axis gave Britain every pretext for intervention: There were reports that Italian planes were bombing areas around the Persian Gulf and that armed German merchant ships were plying Gulf waters. In Teheran, meanwhile, the British and Russian ministers were pressuring my father's government to expel the last German technicians. We were prepared to negotiate this issue too, and had already made concessions. Clearly the British and Russians were not interested: their major objective was the trans-Iranian railroad and on August 23, 1941, both countries invaded without warning.

To the north, strong, motorized Soviet forces crossed the frontier at Azerbaijan; other units advanced in the east at Khorasan and along the whole frontier. Five British divisions came up from the southeast, the south and the west. The Royal Air Force bombed military targets such as Ahvaz, Bandar-Shapur, and Korramshahr, taking pains, however, to avoid petroleum plants. At dawn on August 25, a Royal Navy warship, the H.M.S. *Shoreham*, sank one of our frigates off Abadan; the Soviet Air Force bombarded Tabriz, Ghazvin, Bandar-Pahlavi, Rasht, and Fezajeh.

Our ambassador in Moscow, Mr. Saed, protested to Molotov, and asked him why the Russians had agreed to participate in a military operation against Iran instigated by the British. Molotov did not reply. But we now know that it had been decided to open the Iranian road to Russia when Churchill and Roosevelt met to sign the Atlantic Pact.

On August 28, Reza Shah ordered our forces to lay down their arms. He was notified that on September 17 the allied forces would enter our besieged capital. When he heard that British troops were approaching Teheran, he said to me, "Do you think that I can receive orders from some little English captain?"

He had made up his mind to abdicate. He was too independent and proud a man to subject himself to foreign invaders. The army had stopped fighting and his generals had agreed to disband the armed forces. He knew that meant a resurgence of tribal warfare, for who would keep the country together once he and the army were gone? Above all, he knew how much the British feared and hated him. How could he have dealt with them under such conditions?

The British still ruled the waves in those days. They had India, Iraq, and most of the Middle East. He and I had talked often of British treachery. His distrust of British intentions went back to World War I and to the 1907 partition of the country, which he now felt was being repeated.

On September 16 he abdicated. The abdication act was read to Parliament by the Prime Minister, Furughi:

> I, Shah of Iran by the grace of God and the nation, have taken the grave decision to withdraw and to abdicate in favour of my beloved son, Mohammad Reza Pahlavi. . . .

Parliament ratified the act unanimously. But how was I to reach Parliament in order to swear my oath and receive my investiture? It was not easy. Russian and British troops had just entered Teheran. But crowds of Iranians swelled the streets and thus ensured my triumphant entrance into Parliament. When the ceremony had ended, the Iranians, carried away by their enthusiasm, even wanted to lift up my car and bear it on their shoulders. In this hour of danger, a fantastic display of patriotism and popular loyalty to the dynasty had been shown. This moment, I shall never forget.

The British and Russian ambassadors had remained absent from the ceremony. The British had been inclined to support a Qajar prince who was an officer in the Royal Navy. Only after three days did their governments recognize me. During that time popular demonstrations in my favor showed them that they had no alternative.

The occupying powers hoped to find in me an obedient head of state. They imagined that it would be easy to manipulate so young a sovereign. Their aims were always the same: As in 1907, Iran had to be made into a neutral area, "maintained in a state of respectable anarchy."

My father hoped to go to Canada or to Latin America, but the British would not permit it. A virtual prisoner, he was taken first to India but was not allowed ashore at Bombay. Clearly, the British feared the tremendous impact his presence would have on the already restive subcontinent. Next, they decided to take him to the island of Mauritius and finally to Johannesburg, South Africa. The very last message I received from him in his exile there was on a phonograph record. "My son," he said to me, "fear nothing." I was never to see him again.

When I learned of his death in Johannesburg in 1944, my grief was immense. I owed it to his memory to continue to the very end the task which he had undertaken.

It seemed obvious to me that it was once more a question of the life or death of Iran: We were going back to 1920. But it was 1941 and I was only twenty-two.

Once I was confirmed on the throne by popular support, the British abandoned whatever vague plans they had of putting a prince of the deposed Qajar dynasty in power. I then set about solving the massive problems that arose from the Soviet-British occupation of Iran.

Clearly, the most urgent was some formal agreement with the occupiers that gave legal assurances for Iran's continued independent existence. In January 1942 we concluded a triple alliance with the British and the Russians that recognized Iran's sovereignty and political independence. Article V specified that the Allied forces leave Iranian territory within six months of the end of hostilities. Article VI contained crucial guarantees against any future division of the country between Russia and Britain. This legal framework was only the beginning of the struggle I waged from 1942 to 1946 to keep intact my country's political and economic integrity.

There was little I could do about the all-pervasive black market, a problem that has beset Iran in both war and peace. (Even in the 1970s I was still obliged to battle illegal profiteers and others who moved on the fringes of the economy.) I could merely limit black market operations but there was no hope of breaking its stranglehold on the Iranian economy. That economy, moreover, was further weakened by British and Russian requisitioners who took what they wanted and paid little attention to our needs. Caught between a virulent black market and the demands of the occupying powers, Iran's economy was in shambles.

My leverage was limited but I used what I had. For example, one day the Russian Minister appeared with instructions to dismantle a rifle and a machine gun factory in Teheran and take the equipment to Russia.

"Why should you do that?" I asked. "Why not place an order with us and we will manufacture the guns to your specifications?" Bargaining wasn't easy but in the end I prevailed, mixing stubborn questioning of their right to take the plants with a willingness to put the output at our "ally's" disposal. For we were allies now, Iran had declared war on the Axis.

However, "allied" status did not end foreign interference in our affairs. One day the British ambassador asked me to direct the Central Bank of Iran to print more money to help British and Russian troops defray their local costs. My government had balked, and if the impasse were not resolved, he said, London would lose confidence in the regime. It was, quite simply, a demand that we inflate our currency and add sharply higher prices to the crushing burdens our people already bore. I refused. It was not up to Britain to have confidence in Iran's government but to me, the Parliament, and the people.

It was the first time I had defied an occupying power so dramatically and it helped strengthen my position both at home and with the Allies. However, the British knew how to manipulate Iranian politics and to operate beyond my then limited authority. They controlled elections to the Majles or Parliament—the British used to bring a list of eighty candidates to the Prime Minister in the morning and in the afternoon the Russians brought a list of twelve and that was that—and they got most of what they wanted, pushing our economy into even deeper trouble.

British and Russian interference in our elections was another source of friction and led to my first efforts to bring a man into the government who later would almost destroy me—Mohammed Mossadegh. Thus, in 1943, I asked him to become Prime Minister. I hoped that a "nationalist" leader like Mossadegh would have the backbone needed to reform our electoral system and hold elections free of foreign interference.

To my great surprise, Mossadegh replied that he would accept on three conditions:

1. If the English would agree.
2. If he could see me every morning and hear my advice.
3. If I would give him a personal bodyguard.

I told him I had never asked the English for their advice and that if I were to do so now, I would have to ask the Russians also. I stuck to that position even though Mossadegh said that "nothing was ever done in Iran without the agreement of the British" and the Russians "did not count." I sent my Court Minister, Mr. Ala, to the British and the ex-Cossack, General Yazdan-Panah, to the Russians. The Russians agreed to the proposals; the British did not. In fact, their ambassador told my emissary that "the king is gambling with his crown."

When told of the outcome of these discussions, Mossadegh refused my offer for the Prime Ministership and the farcical elections continued. The English always talk about the merits of democracy, but found it perfectly normal to dictate how Iranian elections should be held.

Mossadegh's reaction should not have surprised me, for he had played a role in Iranian politics long before my father came to power. Indeed, some say that the basis of his fortune, which was considerable, dated back to around 1910. He then, through British influence, was appointed by the Qajar dynasty as finance supervisor in one of our provinces. It is said that he used that position to steal substantial amounts of money. In addition, Mossadegh owned large tracts of land. He also practiced law, having studied in Switzerland and France. In the late 1920s my father made him governor of Azerbaijan province and later he served as ambassador to Iraq. However, we always suspected he was a British agent, a suspicion his future posturing as an anti-British nationalist did not diminish. Certainly my father had long suspected his British connections and in 1940 jailed him on espionage charges. Mossadegh's friends then urged me to intercede for him; this I did and he was released. He said at the time that he owed me his life, but that did not prevent him from betraying me later on.

In November of 1943, Roosevelt, Churchill, and Stalin held one of the key conferences of the war in Teheran, where many of the major decisions affecting the conduct of the war and the postwar future were taken. We were, of course, honored that Teheran had been chosen for this meeting, though we understood the logic behind the choice: Roosevelt and Churchill were already in Cairo, and Teheran was not far from Stalin's home in Georgia.

I had met Churchill the year before when he stopped in Teheran on his way to Moscow. We lunched together in the garden and he talked to me about the importance of radio in the modern world and its usage as an instrument for governing. In fact, he encouraged me to set up a radio network of my own in Iran. We also discussed the war at some length.

Despite my youth I offered my opinions on politics and military matters. I believed that the Allies should invade Europe from the south, that is, through her weakest points, with Italy and the Balkans the most promising targets. Sunk in his chair, with his usual grumpy look, he watched me with interest. He never took his eyes off me while I talked. When I finished he made no comment. Many years later when I read his memoirs, I noticed that the theories I had expounded that afternoon in Teheran coincided with his own.

During the Teheran Conference Churchill lived at the British embassy, several hundred yards from the Russian compound where Stalin and Roosevelt stayed. Although I was technically the host of the conference, the Big Three paid me little notice. We were, after all, what the French called a *quantité negligible* in international affairs and I was a king barely 24 years old. Neither Churchill nor Roosevelt bothered with international protocol that required they call on me, their host. Instead, I paid courtesy visits to both in their embassy residences. Churchill did have some kind words to say about me in the House of Commons on his return to London, but we only talked generalities during our meeting.

Roosevelt stood at the peak of his power that year. Imagine my surprise, when I heard this agreeable man asking me to engage him as a forestry expert in Iran once his term as U.S. President had expired. What could such a request mean? Did Roosevelt believe the future of Iran had been secured so he could already worry about future problems such as reforestration?

While my calls on Churchill and Roosevelt were perfunctory and without real significance, my meeting with Stalin was entirely different. For one thing, he was the only participant who bothered with protocol and called on me, rather than summoning me to the embassy as the other two had done. For another, he was polite, well-mannered, and respectful, not even touching his tea before I had mine. What is more, he spoke about matters important to Iran.

Although I would learn later that Stalin's statements were deceptive, at the time I did not know that. With Molotov sitting beside him and only interpreters present, he began our conversation by declaring: "Have no worry about the next fifty years." Was this a guarantee comparable to the one the Tsars had given the Qajar dynasty, I wondered. As a young patriot king who had seen his country's army destroyed and deprived of weapons and material, I was burning to talk to him about our need for planes and tanks.

When I did, he immediately offered me a tank regiment and a squadron of planes, with troop training and method of delivery to be discussed later. I thanked him warmly for his expression of support, believing that I had taken an important step toward establishing the independence and prestige of my country. It would prove to be my first lesson in Russian duplicity and the hard bargain Moscow drove for every concession. Weeks later the Russian ambassador brought Stalin's terms. They were draconian. Russian officers were to command both the tank regiment and the squadron of planes, at least for the duration of the war. The tank regiment was to be based at Ghazvin, west of Teheran, while the planes would be stationed at Meshed in the northeast of the country. Indignantly, I refused to accept the Soviet conditions. Moscow wasted little time in letting me feel its displeasure. Soviet radio broadcasts began to attack me, while the newspapers of the communist Tudeh party in Iran began to snipe at my handling of foreign affairs.

Earlier than most statesmen, I learned that Moscow plays rough and plays to win. Stalin laid down the rules for the game. However, much as I opposed him and everything he stood for, the man was a colossus. The great victor of World War II was neither Churchill nor Roosevelt, for all their eloquence, but Stalin. He pulled the strings at Teheran, Yalta, and Potsdam, and he imposed a Soviet peace on the world that has now lasted for thirty-five years.

Part of his secret was the willingness to bide his time, while never really pulling back. Moscow saw the moment of opportunity for political action in Iran the day my father was forced to abdicate and leave the country. Moscow helped found the Iranian branch of the communist party, the Tudeh. I say "helped found" because the British had a hand here, too, however difficult that fact may be for naive people to believe. An employee of the Anglo-Iranian Oil Company and a known British agent, Mustafa Fateh, financed the Tudeh newspaper, *Mardom (The People)*. Media ownership, of course, is crucial to any fledgling party's political success and Tudeh was no exception.

Why would the British help launch a communist party abroad? The answer is not that complex. First of all, the British meddle in everything. Second, it was and is their policy to have their people everywhere, hoping to exercise some control no matter what happens. This is a policy Britain has never abandoned, not even today. For example, look at Aden and the rise of communism there. The leaders of the trade unions were all educated in England, at the London School of Economics, I believe.

The British thought that having several people who pretended to be anti-British would give them control of the nationalist movement.

I told the British over and over that it would take only one bullet to put those people away. Once they are gone, what will you do? Who will supervise the trade unions for you? And that is exactly what happened in Aden. Once British agents were eliminated, the whole thing fell into communist hands.

To return to the Tudeh party, the British thought that a hold on the Tudeh would give them similar leverage. Specifically, they hoped to infiltrate their agents among the workers in Abadan and in the refineries and oil fields of the south. Moreover, while Fateh was engaged in publishing *Mardom,* he served as an advisor to the British military attache, General Fraser, and supported his efforts to remove me as commander-in-chief of the army, my greatest source of power. Even in those days the British went to any length to "clip my wings!"

Tudeh did not have much impact at first. It was limited to Teheran teachers and industrial workers, whose economic lot was not very good in those days. Only a few intellectuals supported it. The party had little success in the villages and the countryside; that came only after the war, when Russian interference in our internal affairs mounted dangerously.

At the Potsdam conference in July 1945, Stalin had assured President Truman that Russia would take no action against Iran. Soviet troops were to be out of my country six months after the war with Japan ended; this pledge was reiterated at the London Foreign Ministers' Conference in September of that year. But Stalin had no intention of keeping his promises. Even as he made them, Soviet activities in Iran were being stepped up. Red Army troops stopped Iranian police from entering areas where the Tudeh was strong. Rebellion and unrest were fomented in Azerbaijan and other northern provinces. Allied efforts to make the Russians cease and desist proved futile.

Indeed, Stalin and Molotov were so sure that Iran would fall in their Soviet laps that they rejected a British suggestion to make Azerbaijan, Kurdestan, and Khuzestan autonomous provinces. This proposal was made at the Moscow foreign ministers' conference in December 1945 by Secretary of State James Byrnes and British Foreign Secretary, Ernest Bevin. At first Stalin accepted the proposition, but after Molotov told him to "wait one year and we'll have the whole country," Stalin believed him and refused the Western offer.

For many months it looked as if the Soviet gamble would pay off. Rebellions in Azerbaijan and Kurdistan grew and spread with Russian support. Soviet troops stopped our columns from moving into rebellious areas. In Tabriz, the Soviets pressured the commander of our garrison to surrender to rebel forces. The officer was later tried for treason and condemned to death. I commuted his sentence, however, because I was not sure that he had the means or the will to do anything else, especially since our troops could not get through to end the siege. Still, the fall of Tabriz allowed the rebels to proclaim the autonomy of both Azerbaijan and Kurdistan.

March 2, 1946, came and went without any sign of Russian withdrawal, although they had agreed in London the previous September to leave Iran by that date. Truman sent a polite note to the Russians on March 6. It was ignored. A stiffer letter followed and on March 24 Moscow announced that Soviet troops would pull out. By May the Red Army had officially departed. But the rebellion was far from over and we still had to defend our independence despite the many treaties that guaranteed it. Attempts at secession were made in the west and trouble broke out in the south, notably at Abadan where the Tudeh was still powerful. As if by chance, other tribes rebelled in the Fars, the region of Shiraz and around Isfahan. Clearly, the British and Americans were ready to occupy the south and divide Iran again, should we fail to reclaim our northern provinces. The unrest in the southern regions of the country, however, proved relatively easy to put down so that we could soon turn our full attention to the critical north.

Not surprisingly our relations with Russia during this period were tense. We did not know from one day to the next whether the Soviets would withdraw or turn and attack Teheran, and after they left, if and when they would return to support further rebellions. With our Soviet policy stalemated, my Prime Minister Ebraham Hakimi, an old man of integrity and strongly pro-British sentiments, but always a patriot, resigned. His successor, Ahmed Ghavam, had previously served as Prime Minister. Our relationship had never been an easy one, and it certainly wasn't in 1946. Immediately upon his appointment he left for Moscow and returned with an agreement providing for joint prospecting and extraction of oil, with a 51-49 percent split in Russia's favor.

Fortunately the agreement required parliamentary approval and could thus be held in abeyance. Ghavam's second move, however, could not be ignored as easily. Soon after his return he began talks with the Azerbaijan rebels. One of his proposals called for the promotion of every rebel officer by two grades—making a lieutenant a major, for example—as a price for agreement.

"I would prefer," I said, "to have my hand cut off than to sign such a decree."

The rebels in Azerbaijan at the time were led by a man named Pishevari whom I knew on sight. He had once been elected to our legislature, but Parliament had refused to seat him because he was known to be a communist and a puppet of the Russians. The wisdom of Parliament's action in refusing him a seat was borne out in the rebellion. It now became a matter of taking military action while there was still time. The Russians were gone but not forgotten. Some of Pishevari's rebels had been sent to the Soviet Union for military training. They would return soon, I knew, with equipment, expertise, and Soviet advisors. If I waited any longer, my armies would lose.

Both the government and most of my military leaders strongly advised me against attacking, lest an attack invite Russian intervention. Even the American ambassador, George Allen, who was my friend, warned that "the United States are one hundred percent in agreement with you, but we won't go to war with Russia for your sake." Persuading the opposition to rally round my plans took some months. Ghavam's efforts to settle the rebellion included taking three Tudeh members into the government. Two were given minor posts but one was named Minister of Education. That is and remains a crucial post with enormous influence and I had given my approval with great reluctance. American support for Ghavam complicated my political position that spring. It added to the limits placed on my freedom to maneuver in treacherous political waters and made dismissal of the communist ministers more difficult. Fortunately, they did not remain long in the government. Nevertheless, with Ali Razmara, the chief of staff, behind me, I gathered the needed support, including, in the end, that of the Prime Minister. Moreover, I knew the military operation would not be that risky. The rebels were no better armed than we were and did not enjoy much popular support. Volunteers rushed to our side, more of them in fact than we needed. I felt I had the whole people behind me and preferred to risk an honorable death in battle than to become a monarch of servitude and shame.

The decision made, Razmara and I made repeated reconaissance flights over enemy-held territory, often in old planes, sometimes in a small, twin-engined Beechcraft, and always without radio. As our troops took to the offensive, Pishevari's forces were divided into three columns and harassed increasingly by a loyal local population. Finally, they disbanded and Pishaveri and his acolytes fled across the border into Russia.

This all happened very suddenly. I was in Teheran awaiting the visit of the Russian ambassador. Just before he arrived, I was told that the rebel forces had disbanded and fled. The Soviet envoy then entered, flushed and furious. He demanded an immediate halt to our advance which he termed a "threat to world peace."

I refused, pointing out that our army threatened nothing and no one. We were merely reestablishing the status quo and preparing general elections in territory that belonged to us. Then I simply added, "Besides, you must know that the rebels have just surrendered."

Thus ended the second attempt in the 20th century to erase Iran from the map of the world. The first had been made in the Anglo-Russian Convention of August 30, 1907, that divided the country between Russia and Britain with Russia taking the north and the British the south. It had remained divided until Reza Shah reunited Iran after World War I.

The fact that the same plan was revived to meet Allied needs during World War II shows the continuity of certain western policies toward Iran. The Anglo-American offer to Stalin in Moscow in December 1945 was another step in that direction. Stalin's greed together with his failure to take into account my reaction, the fighting spirit of my ill-equipped soldiers, and the loyalty of our people to crown and country, prevented that plan from succeeding.

Once outside efforts to disrupt our country had failed, politics was used as a means to destroy the state. Corruption and subversion then combined against the nation and the Iranian people whose unity it was my duty to preserve.

Throughout the history of my country outside forces have continually tried to use such tactics. Their sole aim has always been the disintegration of Iran. Time and again such attempts have been made—in 1907 and 1945-46 they did not succeed. Sadly, today they seem to be succeeding.

7

Mossadegh

THE AZERBAIJAN AFFAIR WAS truly a landmark in modern Middle East history. It was in Azerbaijan that the post-war intentions of Stalinist Russia were first exposed. What the Soviet Union did in Azerbaijan, as related in the dramatic debates of the United Nations Security Council, shocked the Free World. It was then that free men everywhere first began to awake to the threat of Communist imperialism.

I think it is fair to say that the cold war really began in Iran. There were of course signs of it elsewhere as well, but the lines were first clearly drawn here. It was in the course of the Azerbaijan affair that America for the first time in history began to play a leading role in the Middle East. Azerbaijan led straight to the Truman doctrine which saved Greece and Turkey from Communist imperialism. It also paved the way for the later Eisenhower doctrine.

After the battle for Azerbaijan, Iran felt a resurgence of true nationalist sentiment. All over the country my people seemed to sense the larger meaning of what had happened. Everywhere they went out of their way to express their loyalty to me.

In 1947 I went to Azerbaijan. My reception in the reunited province—and on my return to Teheran—bordered on hysteria. I shall never be able to forget the enthusiasm and loyalty of the huge crowds that greeted me. The crush of the crowd in Teheran was such that it took us four hours to cover three kilometers.

The Iranian people celebrated our regained national unity. It was the end of a defensive phase in our history and marked the beginning of a constructive one. Elections in July gave Prime Minister Ahmed Ghavam a solid majority in the Majlis and in October he moved to overcome a major obstacle to our freedom of action: the oil agreement he had brought back from Moscow in 1946 when he still hoped negotiation and compromise could end the Azerbaijan uprising.

The agreement called for establishment of a joint Russian-Iranian oil company in which Moscow would retain a controlling 51 percent interest. Fortunately, a 1944 law mandated parliamentary approval of any such accord, allowing us to procrastinate—legally. That Fall, however, Russian patience had run out. The Kremlin pressed hard for passage. On October 22 therefore, Ghavam went before Parliament detailing the agreement and proposing legislation to void it. This frustrated the Russian plan to establish themselves in the north, in the same manner that the British had in the south. The proposal was approved by an overwhelming 109 to 27 vote, with, of all people, Mohammed Mossadegh leading the opposition to a law designed to strengthen Iranian national interests.

The law specified that:

1. All past discussions and negotiations concerning eventual oil concessions to the Soviet government were declared null and void.
2. In the future the Iranian government would refrain from granting concessions to foreign powers for prospecting or extracting oil, no matter what the circumstances.
3. Negotiations with the Anglo-Iranian Oil Company over a larger Iranian share of company profits should begin as soon as possible.
4. If new oil deposits were discovered within the next three years, Iran would be willing to negotiate oil sales to the Soviet Union.

Not surprisingly, Moscow was outraged, and brushed the fourth point aside as insignificant. The situation grew so tense that the Russians threatened to break diplomatic relations. I did not take the threat seriously. Moscow does not easily break such ties. My judgment was confirmed dramatically twenty-five years later when the Kremlin did not respond to President Sadat's expulsion of 16,000 Soviet military advisors. The danger of renewed military intervention faded. Proclamation of the Truman doctrine projected more American power into the Middle East and extended the U.S. military umbrella over Iran. Finally, in early 1948 we began to receive from the United States "light armaments with a view to safeguarding Iran's threatened security."

The stage was set to put Iran on the road to economic growth. Oil production was the key to such development. Despite Tudeh agitation in the oil fields, output expanded steadily: 17 million tons in 1945, 19 million in 1947, 25 million in 1948, with the bulk, of course, sold abroad. I pushed for the drafting of a seven-year development plan. For $3 million we hired an American firm, Overseas Consultants, Inc., to formulate the proposal. They came up with an ambitious $656 million investment scheme geared to agriculture and oil. Expenditures were to be divided as follows:

For the general improvement of social conditions	28.6%
Agriculture	25.0%
Transport	23.7%
Industry and mining	14.3%
Petroleum plants	4.8%
Communications	3.6%

A large part of this budget was to be devoted to hygiene and education. In every province a hospital was planned with between 500 and 700 beds; improvements were to be made in sanitation. Five thousand primary schools, 150 *lycées,* 26 professional schools, as well as technical centers, were to be built. Three new universities were planned for the provinces. A million children and 175,000 adults per year would be attending schools.

Our agriculture was to be mechanized. Canals were to be built as well as about ten dams and hydroelectric power stations. In the field of industry, efforts were to be made to develop metallurgy, textiles, cement and brick works, chemicals, and mining.

More than 3,000 kilometers of new roads, repairs to a further 6,700 kilometers of existing roads, and the building of new railway lines from the capital to Tabriz and from Meshed to Yaza was to improve communications and trading. Our ports on the Gulf and on the Caspian were to be developed, airports were to be built and the postal, telegraphic, and telephonic networks extended.

As usual, politics stymied progress. The Ghavam government fell on December 10, 1947, having failed to survive a no-confidence vote in the Majlis. Over the next thirty months five cabinets came and went. Neither prime ministers nor deputies showed much activity. Time was wasted in fruitless debates which did not produce the money needed to begin our development plan.

In 1948 I made my first trip abroad as a sovereign. I visited Great Britain. King George VI and the royal family showed me such kindness that the trip remains a very happy memory. I had a long conversation with Mr. Bevin, then minister of foreign affairs. As we were speaking of the natural wealth of Iran and I mentioned the region of Kerman, Bevin exclaimed, "Perfect, Kerman! In our zone . . ." "But, it seems to me," I told him "that all of Iran is in the zone of free countries." "It is precisely what I wanted to say," Bevin hastened to answer.

In February 1949 my life was miraculously spared when the mysterious Fakr Arai fired five bullets at me from point-blank range and succeeded only in wounding me in the face and shoulder. Politically, the failed attempt produced positive results: the Tudeh party was outlawed; support for the crown surged. Iranians realized that my death would mean the nation's sinking into murderous chaos, as it has today. Even the religious community, so long at odds with my dynasty and ultimately so influential in my downfall, rallied to my cause. The most eminent doctors of Koranic law called my survival a "true miracle." Since my political leverage had improved, I was able to obtain the Majlis approval for implementation of the seven year development plan. But getting started wasn't easy. We didn't have the money, not even the $25 million our American planners said was needed in start-up costs. In late 1949, therefore, I traveled to Washington for the first time to plead for increased economic and military aid. I received a friendly reception, but returned home empty-handed. In part, the failure of my mission was our fault. The Americans realized we were not handling our internal affairs with sufficient firmness. The recent collapse of Nationalist China had strengthened U.S. determination to aid only those countries who were willing to clean house.

When I returned, I set to work with new energy: I dismissed corrupt officials; I began a program of royal land distribution among peasants. Long-standing defects in our 1906 constitution required correction. The constitution's primary aim had been to establish a constitutional monarchy. Unfortunately, many of its provisions had never been implemented. Thus, by the time I assumed power, my government was operating like an oligarchy: No Senate had been established; the members of the Majlis were able to control the elections and perpetuate themselves in power. In 1949, the Senate was created and met for the first time in 1950. We were subsequently to amend the Constitution to provide the king with power to dissolve the Parliament and order new elections. This enabled us to break the power of the oligarchy. In June 1950 I named my long-time chief of staff, General Ali Razmara, Prime Minister, and he negotiated the first agreement for modest U.S. aid. It wasn't much: some Point IV program money, a small Export-Import Bank loan, nowhere near what we needed to implement our plan. Indeed, a shortage of funds brought most plan activities to a halt. Our American economic advisors left for home. Gradually, popular unrest mounted over the stagnating economy, especially as our efforts to negotiate a better royalty split with the Anglo-Iranian Oil Company were prolonged interminably. The stage was being set for Mohammed Mossadegh. Unhappily, Razmara's Prime Ministership did not work out as well as I had hoped. He could not or would not bring negotiations with the Anglo-Iranian Oil Company to a conclusion. His performance in Parliament was terrible. He failed to articulate clearly the government's positions and was widely perceived as an ineffective parliamentarian. Mossadegh meanwhile, built up his reputation as a spell-binding orator, or more accurately, as a theatrical performer. Had Razmara been sharper, Mossadegh might never have reached the pinnacle he did.

Mossadegh, the orator, is difficult to judge as a politician because of the constant contradiction between his words and acts, and because of his sudden changes of mood from elation to depression before one's very eyes. Whatever his opinions, he was always certain of them and expressed them in hysterical speeches marked with tears and sobbing. He had frequent "diplomatic" illnesses and he played out macabre comedies in which he would exclaim "I am dying..." His fainting spells have become a legend but few know that when he lay on the ground in one of his fits and a doctor opened his vest to see what was wrong he found Mossadegh's hand clutching not his heart but his wallet. He has been compared to Robespierre and to Rienzi, and perhaps most aptly to a character from the Comedia del' Arte.

He called for the nationalization of oil time and again, enflaming the hearts of a people long angered by foreign domination of their affairs. This was an issue on which I had no quarrel with him. But I knew that to function effectively, nationalization had to be coupled or preceded by an agreement with the British. The agreement proved elusive, as we have seen. The Anglo-Iranian Oil Company refused to grant us a fifty-fifty royalty split, similar to the American oil companies' arrangements with Saudi Arabia.

On March 7, 1951, Prime Minister Razmara was assassinated by a member of Fedayeen Islam, a terrorist group of the extreme right, while attending a religious ceremony in the Great Mosque. I can't prove it, but my impression is that Razmara had the agreement with the Anglo-Iranian Oil Company in his pocket when he died. Even if he had, it was too late, for popular indignation was at the boiling point.

I named Hussein Ala, an experienced diplomat and government official, as prime minister. Sadly, it was already too late for moderation and experience. By March 20, both houses of Parliament had passed legislation calling for nationalization of the oil industry. Street riots followed demanding immediate seizure of the installations. Hussein Ala's position rapidly became untenable. Pressure mounted that I name Mossadegh in his stead. On April 28, 1951, I bowed to the inevitable.

It was not an easy decision. I had long been wary of Mossadegh's strident nationalism and violent anti-British sentiments, suspecting that both hid pronounced pro-British statements. His earlier refusal to assume the Prime Ministership during the war, and his support of the Soviet oil treaty had done little to enhance his nationalist credentials. However, he did believe that Britain controlled Iran, his anti-British rhetoric notwithstanding. Still, I worried about that rhetoric and its political effects. Mossadegh was 73 years old and had thirsted for power all his life. Now he had it and he wanted it to be absolute. When we discussed his nomination, I urged prudence and moderation. Our path to political and economic independence was full of pitfalls, I said, and we had to beware of moving too fast. He promised to be cautious. His subsequent actions were, of course, anything but cautious.

Two days after his investiture, Parliament approved a decree seizing the nationalized oil facilities. I approved and signed it, believing Mossadegh would now begin negotiations with the British on a new settlement. This he refused to do for two long years. The initial British reaction was hostile. Paratroopers were ordered to Cyprus. The cruiser H.M.S. *Mauritious* was even then berthed at Abadan. Rumors abounded of naval activities directed towards the Persian Gulf and troop movements along our frontier with Iraq.

"You must realize that I will personally lead my soldiers into battle against you if you attack Iran," I told the British ambassador. My firm stand probably had something to do with the fact that the rumors of war never materialized into action.

Mossadegh refused to bargain, even after the Anglo-Iranian Oil Co. had accepted the idea of nationalization and was ready to negotiate. In fact, when the British government sent the so-called Stokes mission to Teheran it agreed to the fifty-fifty royalty split that had eluded us for so long. Mossadegh refused the offer, just as he later refused the Harriman mission's proposals, and offers of mediation from Churchill, Truman, the World Bank, Eisenhower, and that of an independent tribunal.

For years his political program was based on something he called "negative balance," which ruled out granting any concessions on anything to any foreign power. He hoped to reverse the trend of recent Iranian history, which had been based on the "positive balance," i.e., balancing a concession made to one power with another to a second. The principle was interesting but could not be applied with monomaniac fury to the entire political spectrum. Mossadegh insisted that it could.

He was convinced that the world could not do without Iranian oil, and he was equally certain that Iran could sell her oil without help from abroad. He was wrong on both counts. In response to Mossadegh's intransigence, the Anglo-Iranian Oil Company closed its doors. Royalty payments to the Iranian government were cut off and AIOC blocked sales to others of Iranian oil in which it said it had majority holdings. That meant just about all our oil.

Production at Abadan ground to a halt. Our new organization, the National Iranian Oil Company, had huge oil reserves, but was not equipped to transport or sell them. Small wonder. We didn't own a single tanker, nor did we have even the rudiments of a marketing organization. The British took the case to the International Court of Justice—where the British judge voted for us and the Russian judge absented himself—but Mossadegh refused to recognize the court's authority, even before it ruled that it had no jurisdiction. The dispute then went to the UN Security Council which also failed to resolve it. Mossadegh's messianic and mystical misrule threatened to plunge Iran back into chaos and poverty.

By July 1952 I felt that I could no longer support a man leading the country to its downfall. We had sold no oil since nationalization. There was no agreement in sight and the seven-year development plan was all but abandoned. Opposition to Mossadegh was mounting. On July 13 he demanded extraordinary powers, including the War Ministry. I refused. On July 17 Mossadegh resigned. With some misgivings I named Ahmed Ghavam, a former Prime Minister to succeed him. Although he favored taking strong measures against Mossadegh's left-wing support, he had aged since his earlier government service. He was now an old man, sick, tired, someone who often fell asleep during policy meetings.

Upon Ghavam's appointment, the Tudeh Party and other Mossadegh supporters took to the streets. Mob rule prevailed and Ghavam's government seemed powerless to cope with it. Ghavam then exacerbated the situation with the denunciation of oil nationalization. As the rioting continued, the threat of civil war mounted. I refused to order my troops to fire and was forced to recall Mossadegh and meet his conditions: I named him Prime Minister and Minister of War.

Unfortunately, from then on Mossadegh found these powers more and more convenient to his personal ambitions. He muzzled the press and arrested newspaper editors. Because some of the members of the National Assembly now had the courage to criticize him, Mossadegh reduced that body to impotence, not only by relying on his plenary powers but also by ordering his followers to stay away from the Assembly, thus depriving it of a quorum. Dissenting legislators were also threatened in their homes and on the streets by Mossadegh's hoodlums.

Mossadegh, who had always preached about the danger of depreciating the currency, printed millions of dollars of paper money without any increase in the gold or foreign exchange backing of the currency. He appointed military commanders personally loyal to him, and he allowed—many would say encouraged—the further infiltration of the army by Tudeh communists. He extended martial law. He had Parliament set up a seven-man committee of his followers to study ways and means of curtailing my powers as Commander-in-Chief of the armed forces. The committee actually prepared a detailed report on the subject, which Mossadegh demanded be brought before the whole Parliament. But Parliament refused to pay any attention to the report or to Mossadegh's request; even Kashani and other of Mossadegh's former supporters in Parliament refused to countenance his behavior.

Mossadegh dissolved the Supreme Court. He suspended elections for the National Assembly. Angered because some members of the latter body had been brave enough to oppose him, he announced a national referendum to decide if the current National Assembly should be dissolved. Its members could not help recalling that at the opening of that same session Mossadegh had made a little speech in which he said that 80 percent of them were true representatives of the people.

And for that referendum Mossadegh, the champion of free elections, arranged that those in favor of dissolution and those against it should vote in separate plainly-marked booths! Everyone understood that if a man had the courage to vote against dissolution he would probably be beaten up by Mossadegh's toughs or by those of the Tudeh—actually the two groups by this time were almost indistinguishable. The results were all that Mossadegh—or Hitler before him—could have desired. Dissolution won by over 99 percent of all votes cast. In one provincial town where the entire population was about 3,000 people, 18,000 votes were announced as favoring dissolution. Both in that and in other towns, it seems that the dead rose up to vote!

But in another and grimmer sense many of the dead had voted or tried to vote; for in this and other of Mossadegh's rigged elections literally hundreds of people were killed. By the time of his overthrow, he had had 27 gallows put up on Sepah Square to hang his enemies in public. Some of his intended victims were former members of his own party.

During all his years in Parliament, Mossadegh had posed as a champion of constitutional principles, representative government, and due process of law. He had railed against the idea of marital law and had eulogized free elections and freedom of the press.

But now Mossadegh had in a few months abolished the Senate, dissolved the highest court of the land, and claimed a mandate from the people to eliminate the National Assembly. He had stifled the press, in effect abolished free elections, extended martial law, and tried his best to weaken my constitutional position. What had become of our hard-won constitution of 1906?

According to Mossadegh all of our economic setbacks were part of our fight to free our oil from British domination. He never addressed the fact that the English were still in possession of our oil, uselessly stored, and their possession of it no longer brought us any rent. They simply bought more oil from Iraq and Kuwait, where it cost them less, nine cents per barrel, I believe, compared to thirteen cents for Iranian oil. Thus, Iran lost while Great Britain profited from Mossadegh's negative equilibrium. It began to appear as if Mossadegh's real aim was contrary to what he said. (It must be added that Mossadegh was abandoned by his English friends as soon as he ceased to be of any use, which was as soon as a world oil cartel seemed possible without him.)

As Mossadegh became increasingly entwined in the webs of his own intrigues, he never lost sight of one major aim: the ouster of the Pahlavi dynasty. He had familial ties to the Qajars and had opposed my father's coming to power in 1925. Moreover, he knew that confirmation of his own power depended, in the final analysis, on the loss of mine.

He had a parliamentary commissin study ways of curbing my powers as Commander-in-Chief and was furious when Parliament failed to implement its findings. In February 1953 he attacked more directly, suggesting I leave the country for a while. I felt he should be given the opportunity to implement his own policies and welcomed a respite from his intrigues, so I agreed. The wily Mossadegh then suggested I not leave by air; he felt that crowds protesting my departure might block the airport runway. Instead, he recommended that I drive to the Iraqi border incognito and go from there to Beirut.

But somehow word of our planned departure reached the people, who immediately took to the streets to demonstrate their loyalty to the crown. Heartened by this show of support, I decided to stay.

By mid-year the national mood was changing. Old supporters of Mossadegh dropped away as they realized his policies were opening the way to communist domination of Iran rather then removing British influence. The final crisis broke in late July when he tried to dissolve the Majlis and called for new elections. Political chaos mounted rapidly. The Tudeh again dominated the streets. An uncertain Mossadegh pondered proclaiming a republic with himself as president.

He had already taken more and more power upon himself. A dozen tanks guarded his town house in Teheran while my summer palace at Saadabad had only four, leaving it vulnerable to Tudeh mob attack.

Queen Soraya and I went alternately to live in my father's villa on the Caspian Sea near Rasmar and the hunting lodge at Kelardasht. On August 13, 1953, I decided the time for firm action had come. I signed a decree dismissing Mossadegh and appointing General Fazlollah Zahedi as Prime Minister. Zahedi, a former Mossadegh colleague, had fallen into disfavor and was now in hiding.

I asked Colonel (later General) Nematollah Nassiry, commander of the Imperial Guard, to deliver the messages. His subsequent adventures resembled those of the Three Musketeers.

First, he had to find Zahedi, a man who had been on the run from Mossadegh's police for months, spending each night in different "safe" houses. However, Nassiry quickly located him and delivered my order naming him Prime Minister. Zahedi accepted. Mossadegh was next. Nassiry first arrested three of his close advisors to get some "feel" of his attitude on his dismissal. Soon news of my counter-measures leaked out. Before Nassiry could deliver my message to Mossadegh, communist newspapers hit the streets warning that the Colonel was planning a military coup. At eleven that night Nassiry and two of his officers boldly drove up to Mossadegh's house. It was surrounded by tanks and guards. The colonel and his aides strode past the gun muzzles of the tanks, confident the troops knew him too well to shoot. He was right. Once inside he demanded a meeting with Mossadegh. His aides refused; however, they agreed to deliver my order of dismissal and obtain a signed receipt. Nassiry waited for an hour and a half; then he was handed the receipt. He glanced at the handwriting. It was Mossadegh's. Before he could leave the house, Mossadegh's chief of staff, General Riahi, had him brought to the War Ministry and arrested.

I had already made contingency plans with the help of my American friends, who in those days included Kermit Roosevelt of the CIA and the U.S. ambassador in Teheran, Lloyd Henderson. We had agreed that should Mossadegh use force to resist his ouster, I would temporarily leave the country. We felt my departure would crystallize the situation by forcing Mossadegh to show his true colors and thus rally public opinion behind the throne. To facilitate matters, we had established special radio communications between the Saadabad palace and my two hideaways at Kelardasht and Ramsar. Thus, when Nassiry's driver reached the palace with news of his arrest, the message went out, but for some unexplained reason, the transmission was delayed.

I vividly recall that for two nights I hadn't slept. Well before dawn Mossadegh's radio came on the air, proclaiming that my plan to supersede him had failed. Only a few minutes later Colonel Nassiry's radio message arrived, telling of his imprisonment.

We were at the hunting lodge at Kelardasht when this news reached us. The small airstrip there could only accommodate very small planes, so Queen Soraya and I flew first to Ramsar, twenty minutes away. There we boarded a twin-engined Beechcraft for the flight to Iraq. We were accompanied by two aides—the master of my horses, who had insisted on coming with us, and Major Khatami, who later rose to command our air force and married into my family. I was at the controls. Hours later we landed in Baghdad. Our unexpected arrival was cordially received. The king of Iraq and I were old friends. Nevertheless, Mossadegh's foreign minister, Fatemi, cabled instructions to our ambassador in Baghdad to have me arrested. Incredibly, the man tried to follow these instructions but, of course, to no avail. We spent two days in Baghdad visiting the holy shrines, and then took a commercial flight to Rome. I remembered that I kept a personal car at our embassy there. It is perhaps a measure of Mossadegh's methods that the Charge d'Affaires actually refused to give me the keys to my own automobile. Nevertheless, a trusted embassy employee brought them to me anyway. We stayed in Rome only two days.

The tide had begun turning on August 18. Anti-Mossadegh newspapers managed to publish my decree naming Zahedi Prime Minister and several statements I had made in Baghdad. Later that day the first anti-government demonstrators took to the streets. Nationalists and soldiers moved to break up Tudeh demonstrations. The prisons were stormed. Colonel Nassiry was freed and quickly took command of the Imperial Guards. The next day, August 19, the anti-Mossadegh tide gathered new force. Crowds stormed government ministries and Radio Teheran. At 2 P.M. the radio broadcast information of the Zahedi government. Fighting now erupted around Mossadegh's house. Finally, the prime minister's defenders broke ranks. By nightfall Mossadegh, still dressed in his pajamas, fled over the garden wall of his house into the neighboring garden and took refuge in a cellar belonging to the director of postal services.

I returned to Teheran where I was greeted with popular enthusiasm. Throughout Iran the people were undeniably behind the crown: Before,

I had been no more than a hereditary sovereign, but now I had truly been elected by the people.

In front of his judges, Mossadegh continued to play his part: he was at times pitiable; he fabricated stories and behaved extravagantly. He continued to make a spectacle of himself in front of the international press. I knew that he would certainly be condemned to death, for he had been convicted of treason. I therefore instructed the court not to take into account his actions against me.

After three years in prison, Mossadegh was freed. He went into retirement on his large estate at Ahmad-Abad to the west of Teheran and died there in 1967. I was unable to prevent the execution of Hossein Fatemi, Mossadegh's Foreign Minister, because he was a communist. However, I personally have provided for the financial well-being of his family. This support was suspended when Mrs. Fatemi, who had been living in London, recently returned to Iran in support of Khomeini.

The trials which followed the end of Mossadegh's rule revealed the events of 1951-53 in a strange light. For instance, it turned out that when Mossadegh took control of the War Ministry in 1951, only 110 officers were members of the Tudeh Party, whereas 640 officers were members by the time he fell in 1953.

The Communists had planned first to use Mossadegh to topple me. Second, uncovered Tudeh papers revealed that Mossadegh was to be eliminated two weeks after my departure. I have seen postage stamps printed in the name of the People's Iranian Republic which was then to be proclaimed. The uprising of the masses in my favor took the conspirators by surprise. Aware that the people were not behind them, the Tudeh went underground. It should not be forgotten that Stalin had died a few months before and that the Soviet strategy was to undergo some considerable changes.

Since there was no doubt that the Russians had supported Tudeh politically and financially, the world media credited Great Britain and the U.S. with financing the overthrow of Mossadegh. But the most accurate documentation proves that at the time of these events the CIA had spent no more than $60,000. I reallv do not think that such a sum is enough to make a whole country rise up in a few days.

In May 1957, President Eisenhower, in an address to the American people, affirmed the threat of communism that my nation faced under Mossadegh. He stated: "Under the courageous leadership of the Shah, the people of Iran met that danger. In their effort to restore economic stability, they received indispensable help from us. . . . Iran remains free. And its freedom continues to prove of vital importance to our freedom."

It took nearly thirty months for the Iranian people to see Mossadegh as the prototype sorcerer's apprentice, incapable of controlling or dominating the forces of destruction which he himself had unleased.

In the beginning he had served his country well. In his negative way he had crystallized our people's anti-foreign sentiments; with his own interests at heart he had jumped on the bandwagon of xenophobia. Oddly enough, his real usefulness to the country ended with his appointment as Prime Minister. In any country a head of government to be effective must do something positive. Mossadegh—let us hope unintentionally—betrayed the common people of Iran by promising them a better deal and then sabotaging his own promises. The people lived for a time on these promises. Then they realized that no matter how dramatically promises are put, you cannot feed your children upon them. They also saw that their native country was disintegrating before their eyes. So the people, especially the common people, rebelled. Mossadegh left the country ruined and in debt. The damages suffered by our economy amounted to hundreds of millions of dollars and three wasted years.

We shall see in the following chapter how the oil question was settled.

8

From the Age of Petroleum to the Atomic Age

THE DEVELOPMENT OF THE oil industry constitutes the most tumultuous aspect of modern Mideast history. It is an unending series of intrigues, plots, political and economic upsets, acts of terrorism, *coups d'état* and bloody revolutions. To understand the upheaval in Iran and other parts of the Middle East, one must understand the politics of oil.

The world petroleum story is one of the most inhuman known to man: in it, elementary moral and social principles are mocked. If powerful oil trusts no longer despoil and humiliate our country it is not because these predators have become human, but because we have won a hard-fought battle which has been waged since the beginning of the century.

In 1901 the rights for the exploration, prospecting, exploiting, refining, transporting, and selling of oil in all of Iran, with the exception of five northern provinces, were accorded to William Knox D'Arcy. D'Arcy's company was to refund 16 percent of the benefits to the Iranian government. Our government could not intervene in the company's affairs and only unskilled Iranians were to be employed by the company.

D'Arcy's company went through several reorganizations in order to remain financially solvent and in 1909 became the Anglo-Persian Oil Company (later known as the Anglo-Iranian Oil Company [A.I.O.C.]

and then as the British Petroleum Company). War clouds had been gathering in Europe, and as early as 1912 the British government had become much concerned about petroleum supplies. Winston Churchill, then First Lord of the Admiralty, recommended that to meet naval needs his government acquire a 51 percent interest in the Anglo-Persian Oil Company. A law to this effect was approved by the British Parliament only six days before the outbreak of war in August 1914. In 1920 the Qajar government worked out a new agreement with Anglo-Persian which represented a slight gain for my country. Interestingly enough, Sir Sydney Armitage-Smith, a British treasury official, acted as negotiator for the Persians.

In 1933, the Iranian government managed to repeal this agreement. A new accord was concluded which guaranteed somewhat more revenue for Iran. More importantly, the surface area covered by the concession was reduced to a hundred thousand square miles and the company was required to employ Iranians in preference to other nationalities.

Profits from the Anglo-Iranian had soared. The initial investment of some 100 million dollars had been completely recovered by the beginning of the twenties. Subsequently, according to the most reasonable estimates, the company's income reached twenty-five times this sum. Iran was getting nothing from the prodigious wealth drawn from her soil. It all went to the company's shareholders, of which the largest were the British Admiralty—the Royal Navy was run on Iranian oil—and the British Treasury. So by 1950, Iran had received 45 million dollars of royalties for her own oil, while the A.I.O.C. paid 112 million dollars in *income tax* to the British government. This gives some idea of the size of the dividends paid to shareholders.

The company's attitude was, furthermore, curiously discriminating with regard to our country since it paid higher royalties to other countries, including both Iraq and Kuwait. In addition, the gas extracted with the oil was entirely wasted and burned on the spot. The clauses of the new 1933 agreement were not respected: the company failed to train Iranian technicians and consequently refused to reduce the number of foreign employees; they paid miserable salaries to the Iranians and failed to lodge them decently and in accordance with the agreement.

Whereas American companies had already signed a 50-50 contract with Saudi Arabia, the royalties paid by the Anglo-Iranian represented less than 30 percent. Finally, a large part of the profits gained at the expense of Iran were invested in prospecting and digging for oil in other countries so that humiliation was added to injustice.

In May 1951 the law to nationalize the oil industry was ratified. I was one of the most ardent supporters of this nationalization. However, I felt that this act had to be followed or preceded by negotiations. Unfortunately, the very opposite occurred, due to Mossadegh's recalcitrance.

Great Britain protested, sent the dispute to the International Court of Justice in The Hague, withdrew its 4,800 technicians from Abadan and decreed an oil blockade of our ports. The National Iranian Oil Company (N.I.O.C.), which was formed immediately after nationalization, could not sell a barrel of oil even at half price due to this blockade. Thus Iranian oil remained in the barrels and the reservoirs for three years, constituting a liability rather than an asset since we had to maintain the closed installations. After Mossadegh was deposed, we were able to resume sensible oil negotiations.

I had no intention of tampering with the 1951 oil nationalization law. Mossadegh and I had agreed in principle on the nationalization of oil, but had disagreed on its implementation. One of my post-Mossadegh aims was the relaxation of British control of our oil industry. A more conciliatory approach in 1951 might have achieved this. But by 1954 this effort had been immensely complicated by the British stranglehold on our oil supply lines. Only as a result of lengthy negotiations were we able to reach a basic agreement with a Consortium of the eight largest oil companies in the world. Our National Iranian Oil Company, as owner, employed the Consortium as its contract agent for the operation of the fields and sale of the oil. The agreement was valid for 25 years (with an option for three five-year extensions) and gave Iran 50 percent of the profits. At that time, President Eisenhower sent me a letter expressing his personal appreciation for my efforts in resolving the oil problems caused by Mossadegh's government.

Through the passage of the Iran Petroleum Act in 1957, we were able to reduce the Consortium's power in our oil industry. This act allowed more foreign companies into the country and expanded the activities of the N.I.O.C. into every phase of oil production in the country. The Irano-Italian Oil Co., formed with the E.N.I. of Enrico Mattei, and later the Iran Pan-American Oil Company (I.P.A.C.), formed with the Pan American Oil Company, were examples of these arrangements—both concerned new areas for prospecting.

These arrangements, which provided for a 50-50 participation, accomplished two important goals. First, they enabled N.I.O.C. to share for the first time in the management of our oil fields. Second, they enabled us to obtain a larger share of the profits, since the foreign company's profit was subject to a 50 percent income tax. Iran's true share was 75 percent. These innovative accords changed the course of the oil industry in the Mideast as well as other areas. They paved the way for the exploited nations to gain greater control of their own wealth.

The great bulk of our oil production, however, was managed by the consortium under our 1954 agreement. In 1958 I undertook to change this. My aim was that N.I.O.C. take control of our oil fields, in fact as well as in name, by assuming full management responsibility. These efforts consumed a fifteen year period—a period in which I would come to understand the perils that await those who tamper with the oil magnates. Finally, I won out—72 years of foreign control of the operation of our oil industry was ended on July 31, 1973.

On that date the Consortium became in effect a simple buyer of such crude Iranian oil as we wanted to sell them. The N.I.O.C. took command of all activities including running the refinery in Abadan and it was henceforth up to the N.I.O.C. to plan the exploration of geological beds in the interest of the nation.

From the instant in 1957 when I set Iran on the course of independence, strange happenings began to take place. Deplorable events followed this truly revolutionary step in the history of oil since enormous interests were at stake.

I believe that Enrico Mattei, the general director of the A.G.I.P., was among the first casualties. When I knew him, engineer Mattei was a man in his fifties with extraordinary dynamism and an admirable knowledge of the petroleum world. He was fully aware of the risks he was taking in defying the great international cartels. And he always said that he did not have time to be afraid. To save time, he constantly traveled by plane or helicopter. His two-motor Marane-Saunier 760 was always piloted by the excellent and very prudent Major Irnerio Bertuzzi.

On October 27, 1962, at 5:25 P.M., the plane took off from the Sicilian airport of Catania and was to land in Milan at 6:57. William McHale, the head of the Italian service of the American journal *Time,* accompanied Mattei. At 6:55 the control tower of the airport received a last message from Bertuzzi, who was preparing to land, and nothing after that.

About 10:00 P.M. it was learned that the plane had fallen in flames near Bascape in the province of Pavia. There were no survivors. The accident was officially termed as one "due to lack of visibility."

I have never believed that Mattei's death was an accident. Earlier that month, during an inspection of the Marane plane, an explosive device had been found hidden in one of the motors.

From the moment that Iran became the master of its own underground wealth, a systematic campaign of denigration was begun concerning my government and my person in certain of the mass media. It was at this time that I became a despot, an oppressor, a tyrant. Suddenly malicious propaganda became apparent; professional agitators operating under the guise of "student" organizations appeared. This campaign, begun in 1958, reached a peak in 1961. Our White Revolution halted it temporarily. But it was begun anew with greater vigor in 1975 and increased until my departure.

In response to my call the ministers of OPEC met in Teheran on December 22 and 23, 1973. This assembly decided to raise the price of each barrel of oil from 5.032 to 11.651 dollars.

Earlier that year during the Arab oil embargo, we had sold oil on the spot market for $35 a barrel. That told us something: Demand for oil was so strong that price was no object. Oil had been underpriced for far too long. It was time to move firmly and with dispatch. I was also convinced that in the long run the world economy would be healthier when oil sold at a price which would foster exploration of other forms of energy.

Early in the decade, President Nixon and Secretary of State Kissinger wrote urging that we rescind the announced increases. This correspondence continued through the end of President Ford's administration.

It was to me an economic aberration, that oil remained much cheaper than Evian mineral water, for oil is a noble product from which some 70,000 different products are derived. Among these, many thousands have been developed in such a way that the cost of petroleum is only a small percentage of the total cost. In my opinion, oil should, therefore, become the primary substance of an increasingly diversified and sophisticated petrochemistry. The use of oil for heat, light, or railroads is a wasteful policy with little thought for the future. This is a philosophy of *Après nous les déluges!*

As I explained in 1973, the sale of oil at its equitable price is in the real interest of all industrialized countries. By raising oil prices in stages to levels which would allow competition from other costly forms of energy, one would achieve a more sophisticated use of petroleum and at the same time an augmentation of the energy reserves of the world.

A policy of petroleum at its just price requires not only the periodic revision of the price but also cooperation with consumer countries, especially with the Organization of Economic Cooperation and Development (O.E.C.D.), in order to avoid the creation of an inflationary spiral of international prices. Through negotiation one should be able to fix periodically, by common agreement, the price of energy upon which the industry of the future world could be constructed.

International pressure groups immediately launched a malicious campaign against me through the mass media. I was accused of attempting the disintegration of the West's economy. Not surprisingly, little attention was paid to my full program. They ignored the proposal I had made to the consumer states: to limit their taxes on oil to 100 percent of the purchase price. For, in effect, the public treasuries of the consumer nations have collected a higher tax per gallon than the sale price of the producer countries.

During my remaining years in the country, the National Iranian Oil Company grew and prospered. Oil revenues topped $22 billion in 1977. We engaged in building refineries in Asia and Africa and in various offshore ventures.

Far from being the OPEC price hawk depicted in the West, within the cartel I counseled moderation towards an ordered and rational growth. After 1975-76 I repeatedly attempted to keep oil prices in check and to persuade my partners that price advances should be gradual and fitted to world economic conditions.

In 1977, for example, I agreed with Western requests to freeze oil prices in 1978. U.S. Secretary of State Cyrus Vance and British Foreign Secretary David Owen approached me during a break in a CENTO meeting in Teheran and asked me to hold the line. Interestingly enough, Vance urged a freeze extending beyond 1978. Owen did not. Confident that North Sea oil would soon make Britain independent of imports and quite probably a net exporter, he was only anxious for a bridging agreement that would take his country—and presumably his Labor government—through the next year. We were alone in a room of my palace during a reception when the request was made. I told them sure, why not? And that was that.

Iran then was the world's fourth largest producer, with a daily output of around 6 million barrels, and the second largest exporter. In addition to the National Iranian Oil Company, we had a National Society for Petrochemical Industries with eleven companies and factories. The National Society of Iranian Gas handled drilling and distribution of our huge natural gas reserves—the equivalent of the Soviet Union's—and continued to look for new deposits. We know that many gas deposits in Iran still wait to be discovered.

Not surprisingly, many of the ideas I put forward in 1973-74 have now been accepted by major Western institutions.

In March 1979, the French newspaper *Le Monde,* which had consistently attacked my policies, published in its "diplomatic" supplement a long study entitled "The Crisis of Energy and the Price of Oil." This article, coming five years and three months after the Teheran conference, took up nearly all the arguments which I had advanced in favor of a just price for petroleum, arguing that it was a question *of necessity* which all countries have been too slow to admit. The article pointed to the scandal that 120 billion cubic meters of gas continued to be burned off each year as sheer loss in the world. It established once again the fact that the part appropriated by public treasuries from the price of the sale of oil to consumers is more than the cost of the oil. Finally, it arrived at the same conclusions concerning the necessity for an international agreement.

In all of these studies there is not a single word, not a single reference to the 1973 O.P.E.C. meeting in Teheran. The author relies first of all on a study made in 1976 by the Continental Oil Company, establishing the fact that the price of a barrel should rise from 24 to 27 dollars (1975) in order to allow the five sources of energy to enter into competition with oil; and secondly on a report made in 1978 by the Rand Corporation for the CIA. This report emphasizes that "the increase of the price of oil up to 'thirty dollars' (constant) per barrel would allow the proven oil reserves of the world to be doubled."

I should add that at the beginning of August 1978, Mr. James Schlesinger, U.S. Secretary of Energy, declared that the price of oil could rise to 40 or 50 dollars a barrel.

Thus, my policy, which had been denounced as that of "destabilization," and "shameless blackmail," when it was proposed, became the only world-wide policy possible.

9

The White Revolution

IN THE SECOND YEAR of my reign, when war was still raging and we were faced with acute problems, I declared a five-point program to assure the minimum needs of every citizen: health, food, clothing, housing and education for all.

Since then, at every opportune moment, I have reiterated these aims and stressed the necessity of implementing them. If our nation wished to remain in the circle of dynamic, progressive and free nations of the world, it had no alternative but to completely alter the archaic order of society, and to structure its future on a new order compatible with the vision and needs of the day. This required a deep and fundamental revolution which would put an end to injustice, tyranny, exploitation, and reactionary forces which impeded progress. This revolution had to be based on spiritual principles and religious beliefs, and the preservation of individual and social freedoms.

To realize these goals it was essential that land reform should take place and the feudal landlord-and-peasant system be abolished; that the relationship between workers and employers should be regulated so that labor should not feel exploited; that women—who after all make up half the population—should be treated as equals no longer legally categorized with lunatics and criminals; that the scourge of illiteracy should be removed; that no one should die of disease nor live in misery and wretchedness through lack of treatment or care; that backwardness in the villages should be ended; that the undeveloped outer regions should be connected with the rest of the nation; and in general, that conditions in harmony with today's civilized world should prevail.

With these aims in mind, in January 1963 I presented to my people the first stage of my White Revolution.* This program would construct a modern and progressive Iran on sound and strong foundations, so that my presence would no longer affect the destiny of the country. At that time, I received a personal note of congratulations from President Kennedy on my White Revolution. Upon my visit to the United States, in August 1967, President Johnson also declared: "The changes in Iran represent very genuine progress. Through your White Revolution," Johnson continued, "Iran has risen to the challenge of new times and new generations . . . without violence, and without any bloodshed."

More than half the arable land of Iran belonged to private owners, of whom perhaps not more than thirty (some of them tribal khans) owned 40 villages or more. These landowners, who spent most of their time in Teheran or abroad, rarely resided on their estates, and had little interest in improving the agricultural and social conditions of the peasants who lived on them. They appointed agents to manage their landholdings. Unfortunately, these agents' primary aim was their own financial gain. Thus, the peasants who worked these lands were often exploited.

In order to change this land ownership system, in 1950 I issued a decree which would have distributed the Crown estates—more than 2,000 hamlets and villages that belonged personally to me—to the peasants. However, the Mossadegh government opposed any changes in the existing system of land tenure—Mossadegh himself was a large landowner. He stopped this distribution of Crown lands, and the program could only be implemented after his fall. By the time the program was completed, toward the end of 1958, more than 500,000 acres of Crown lands were shared among more than 25,000 farmers. In spite of these efforts, the main task, that of breaking up the big private estates, remained uncompleted. Finally, in January 1963, a new law was passed by plebiscite which limited private ownership of arable land. This was the First Principle of my White Revolution.

---

*See Appendix I for full chronological listing of White Revolution Principles.

Agrarian reform was carried out in three stages. First, no landowner could own more than one village. Peasants who worked the land had the right to buy the surplus with loans repayable over 15 years. Landowners were paid in shares of state-owned industries.

The second stage of the reform provided that landowners who did not personally cultivate their lands had to rent them for 30 years or to sell them to those who did.

Finally, in the third stage, landowners who had rented out lands had to share the income with the farmer or sell him the area he cultivated. Large landowners could only keep untilled land suitable for mechanized farming. I am against the exploitation of man by man, but not against the exploitation of machinery by man. To finance our land reforms, we sold shares in government-owned factories. This law, the Third Principle of our White Revolution, not only complemented our land reform program, but enabled the public to participate more fully in Iran's economic affairs.

Our other methods of financing this land reform and our innovations in agricultural management—our agricultural banks, rural cooperatives, and our corporate farm ventures in which the farmer exchanged land for shares—have been detailed elsewhere.*

At the inception of our land reforms that January, I had predicted that the forces of the clergy (the Black reaction) and the communists (the Red destruction) would attempt to sabotage this program: the former, because they wished the nation to remain submerged in abject poverty and injustice; the latter, because their aim was the complete disintegration of the country.

My prophecy was fulfilled. Widespread sabotage began, accompanied by murder and rioting, the most severe outbreaks of which were the rebellion in the south of the country and the disorders in Teheran in June 1963.

These revolts were financed by large landowners angered by their failure to block agrarian reform. Although the confounded alliance of the Red and the Black—that is, of the revolutionary left and the most extreme religious reactionaries—had been outlined in Mossadegh's day, in 1963 an organized Islamic Marxist movement still was only a spectre.

---

*See M. R. Pahlavi, *White Revolution,* translated from the Persian and published by the Imperial Pahlavi Library, 1967, and George Lenczowski, *Iran Under the Pahlavis.* Hoover Institution Press, Stanford, 1978.

Only in the late seventies would Iran and my government experience fully the wrath of this unholy alliance.

The 1963 Teheran riots were inspired by an obscure individual who claimed to be a religious leader, Ruhollah Khomeini. It was certain, however, that he had secret dealings with foreign agents. Later the radio stations run by atheist *émigrés* belonging to the Tudeh Party accorded him the religious title of Ayatollah ("the sign of God") and praised him to the skies, although he was anything but divinely inspired. These events were, in fact, a repetition of those that had occurred in Khorasan during my father's reign, following the move to modernize men's clothing. On that occasion the instigator was an adventurer whom nobody knew and who later was discovered to be a foreigner. Khomeini was neither arrested nor tried for his incendiary activities. He was simply exiled—first to Turkey, then to Iraq.

The vast majority of the country's religious leaders, its real spiritual leaders, played absolutely no part in these events. The riots were financed by a group of landowners affected by the land reform law. The thugs who took part attacked defenseless women in the streets of Teheran, smashed buses taking children to school, set fire to the public library, destroyed a sports stadium and looted shops.

By the time the third stage of our agrarian reform had been implemented, there remained very few large landowners. In effect 2½ million peasant families had become owners of the land on which they worked. Undeniably, this White Revolution was not to the taste of the large landowners or clergy. However, land tenure reforms could not solve all Iran's agrarian problems.

Unfortunately, Iran has few forests: 13,000 square miles in the north along the Caspian and the northern slopes of the Alburz Mountains and another 5-7.5 million acres scattered and dispersed in the west and southwest, around the central desert and along the banks of the Sea of Oman. Moreover, only a part of these forests—3.3 million acres—is suitable for forest industries. The rest, ravaged in the past, does not possess immediate economic value.

From antiquity until the 18th century, Iran was particularly rich in forests of oaks, wild almonds, pistachios, and in the south, conifers. Throughout the ancient history of Persia there is no trace of the private ownership of forests. Islam teaches that streams and rivers, forests and grazing fields, and ponds and marshes can never become private property. It was during "feudal" periods, when the central power was weak or corrupt, that the big landowners seized vast regions that were wooded. I declared in 1963 that:

"The forest is natural wealth to whose creation and development no person has contributed. Therefore it is only just that it should belong to all the inhabitants of the country."

Iran possesses 30,000 square miles of pastures of good or intermediate quality and 38,000 square miles of wooded prairies. Unfortunately these pastures can only provide food for about one half of the existing flocks. Thus, the meadows are exhausted and destroyed rapidly and the animals remain lean. This scarcity of good pasture had produced numerous abuses: renting of land at prohibitive prices, refusal to rent to cattle breeders, and the usage of meadows for more lucrative ends.

After nationalization, conservation, development and cultivation of the forests became the responsibility of the Organization of Forests of Iran. To rehabilitate the forests which were destroyed, vast areas were prohibited for commercial use, and the making of charcoal was banned. The National Iranian Oil Company opened thousands of centers where fuel, kerosene, and petroleum could be purchased to take the place of charcoal. Thus the forests of the north were sufficient to provide the 200,000 tons of charcoal required for the whole country as well as the million cubic meters of wood that our industries consumed.

Finally, more than 9 million trees were replanted in 26 regions, creating 70,000 acres of "green belts" around cities and on the borders of the major highways. Numerous national parks were established and 98,000 acres of new forests and 250,000 acres of various types of vegetation and trees were planted to limit the advance of the desert. These constituted the first steps on the way to restoring our dilapidated natural resources.

As for pastures, they were placed at the disposal of the cattle breeders. The minister of agriculture undertook a program of development of the pastures and multiplication of wells, drinking troughs and shelter.

In 1968, we focused our attention on the nationalization of our waters, both surface and subterranean. According to the Holy Koran, water belongs to everyone. Unfortunately Iran has always lacked water. While the average annual rainfall for the whole planet is 860 mm., Iran only receives 231 mm.; and depending on whether the year is dry or wet, our water resources vary between 280 and 520 billion cubic meters—an average of 378 billion cubic meters.

Seventy-three percent of our rainfall is absorbed by our irrigated land or is lost in lakes and seas. One hundred three billion cubic meters on the average is available in rivers and springs. Our annual consumption in 1976 was about 90 percent of this figure. Obviously, just one dry year creates a dangerous water shortage. Two successive dry years mean catastrophe. This fact, together with our rapidly rising population, the extension of agriculture, the development of steel mills and petrochemical industries and finally the increased requirements for electrical energy, mandated a policy of water conservation.

Before August 1953 five small dams had been constructed. They were followed by eight large ones. Altogether 13 billion cubic meters of water allowed 2 million acres, of which half was new land, to be cultivated and to produce 1,804 MGW of electricity. When I left Iran, five other dams were under construction. Studies were underway on the feasibility of obtaining water contained in underground limestone formations. Our water resources were also to be augmented through desalinization of sea water by means of nuclear reactors on the border of the Persian Gulf.

I envisioned for the distant future, irrigation of 37.5 million acres in place of 5.6 million today. In order to achieve this end it was necessary to produce more energy. Now, even if it were possible in principle to produce around 10,000 MGW from the water sources of the dams of Iran, we would still not be there!

From 1963 to 1977, production of electric energy increased from 2.3 billion to more than 20 billion KWH, the capacity of our electric plants from 850 MGW to more than 7,500. To this would soon be added 2,500 MGW to be produced by the two nuclear plants under construction. The final goal was the production of 25,000 MGW of atomic electrical energy.

If I am accused of neglecting agriculture, it is the reverse which is true. In a country lacking sufficient moisture and humus, the investment necessary to irrigate and enrich the soil was of course considerable and it would have been difficult to do more than we did.

A similar revolution was to occur in the commercial area—and the wealthy entrepreneurs would decry these reforms as well. The revolution began in 1963 when the Fourth Principle of the White Revolution—profit sharing for workers—was adopted. In its implementation, this law became one of the most progressive of its type in the world.

Under its terms, employers were obliged to conclude collective agreements that provided:*

1. Payment of bonuses based on higher productivity or reductions in operating costs;
2. Payment to the workers of a part of the net profit.

A special bank geared to the needs of salaried workers made low-interest loans of 4 percent a year—for home improvements and debt consolidation. Close cooperation between labor and management was encouraged.

Three major principles governed our labor legislation:

1. Every Iranian has a right to employment. A jobless worker would receive unemployment compensation equivalent to his minimum guaranteed income until employment offices had found him another job;
2. The minimum wage for unskilled labor went up in direct proportion to the cost of living;
3. Productivity schedules provided higher pay for higher individual output.

As important as all these steps were, they remained only a beginning. Our concept of democratic equality included economic equality. Consequently, workers should become co-owners of the factories and workshops which employed them. For, after all, these businesses functioned only thanks to their efforts.

In August 1975, the Thirteenth Principle of our Revolution was enacted into law. All private units of production which had existed more than five years were required to sell 49 percent of their shares to their own workers and employees. Newly constructed state-owned industries were to distribute 99 percent of their shares to the general public.

This principle completed the democratic economy and was to constitute a turning point in the industrial, economic and social evolution of Iran. The association of all the working population, with the capital of the major units of production, was to cement the union between owners, technicians and workers. A resurgence of the feudal capitalism which

*During 1976, 530,000 workers in the public and private sectors were paid bonus/profit-sharing benefits of about 12 billion rials—equivalent to one or two months' salary per person. From the law's inception in 1963 to 1975, the total sum of net profits paid to workers had multiplied by a factor of 128.

had oppressed our nation at the beginning of the century became impossible.

At first, of course, we heard cries of "Sacrilege!" from some factory owners. A year later, however, the majority of owners initially affected by this legislation admitted that their enterprises had never before been so profitable. They had to agree that our reforms cost them nothing because the increase in productivity had raised the profits to a level that made the owners' reduced percentages equal to their previous profits. One hundred fifty-three industrial enterprises, held by a small number of shareholders, had sold their shares to 163,000 workers and peasants. Transactions were underway concerning 320 large firms which were to sell shares estimated at 170 billion rials.

In every case the purchase of shares was made possible by government loans. The Council for the Expansion of the Ownership of Units of Production provided the necessary credit, which was repaid through 10-year loan plans directly deducted from the dividends of the shares.

The following figures are indicative of the success of this program:

Fifteen years ago a worker made on the average 2,000 rials, or less than $30 a month. No more. In 1978 the salary of a worker without particular qualifications was 10,000 rials, to which must be added 20 percent of the profits of the firm and where the law of August 1975 was vigorously applied, dividends from the acquired shares.* Moreover, low cost housing was available to workers. Food was cheap because the five basic food stuffs (meat, sugar, oil, rice and bread) were subsidized throughout Iran, and in addition special fixed-price food stores were set up especially for workers.

I understand that many of these shops were burned with the arrival of the so-called Islamic Republic.

The sale of shares of public-sector factories, except basic industries such as copper, steel, coal, oil, railroads and armaments, was scheduled for October 1978. Unfortunately, the rioting and pillaging of the insurgents which began in September of 1978 and continued until my departure stymied the implementation of this plan

In spite of these economic advances, a vast gulf still separated the peasants from the large landowners.

---

*For example, when I visited a sugar factory near Quchan in 1973, I learned that 80 percent of the workers owned cars and 50 percent employed household help.

The peasant, being at once poor, ignorant and often illiterate, lived far from the towns where justice was administered. Thus, he had little hope of obtaining justice that would be both equitable and inexpensive.

The ordinary legal problems of the peasant concerned first of all his plot of land and then perhaps the few differences he might have with other farmers concerning the fields, water, animals or instruments used in his work. The sums involved did not usually amount to more than the value of a cow or a sheep or a few acres of arable land. Now, in order to settle these questions, he had to file a complaint, which meant acquiring the services of a lawyer in town, and then to travel one or more times to the inferior court, often situated at some distance. The summoning procedure also required an appearance at the prefecture, a process of appeal, and a journey to Teheran where the court was located.

Meanwhile the courts were filled with thousands of these small cases, most of which were not worth the time and cost to the nation. Furthermore, the peasants were not in the habit of solving their differences by legal means. They took recourse to ruse, sometimes to violence, and vengeance, which would aggravate the situation and often end with the intervention of the state police.

The logical solution seemed to me to be the most simple one: the peasant would not go to the law; instead, the law would go to the peasant, and to his own village. A local villager could better understand and solve the problems of another villager. What a distinguished jurist from the city might grasp only with difficulty from a pile of papers, an old villager on the location could understand perfectly and resolve wisely, for he would know the antecedents of the case and the roots of the litigation. And he spoke the same language as the litigants.

I felt that the peasants would be quite willing to have local juridical problems settled by persons whom they knew and respected. In this way, the peasant would waste neither time, nor money, nor energy. The burden on the court system and the public treasury would be lightened as well.

The first House of Equity was installed on an experimental basis in December 1963 in the village of Mehia near Isfahan. It was followed by a hundred others and institutionalized by the Ninth Principle of the White Revolution, in October 1965. At the end of 1977, there were 10,358 Houses serving 19,000 villages throughout the provinces, with a total population of more than ten million.

The House of Equity was actually a court of village justice. The judges, who were five in number, were chosen for three years by the villagers themselves from among people locally respected. The government did not appoint them. Since the position was honorary, justice was free of charge to the litigants.

The judges were not bound to complicated or useless procedures. They were free to summon or to visit the litigants, to hear witnesses, proceed to verify their testimony, and obtain the opinion of experts.

The success of the House of Equity was immediate and spectacular. In 1965 they settled 18,000 cases to the satisfaction of everyone. The statistics, which stop at the end of 1977, indicate that 3 million differences had been resolved. If these cases had been adjudicated through the established judiciary, they would have required years to settle and would have been substantially more costly to the government and the litigants.

The quality of the justice obtained in the Houses of Equity was outstanding. In the view of numerous legal experts, the decisions of these common magistrates were always well reasoned, just and logical. This performance by simple villagers astonished the most eminent jurists. I myself was less surprised by it. In visiting the peasants, I often posed questions concerning the operations of the Houses of Equity. Without fail, the peasants informed me that their opinions were always solicited and given serious consideration.

In July 1966 we extended this institution to the cities, where minor differences among the citizenry were not lacking. Councils of Arbitration in the towns were also comprised of five arbitrators chosen for three years by the inhabitants of each quarter.

An advisor, selected from among acting or retired judges, lawyers or notaries, provided advice in matters of juridical rules if so requested, but the final decision rested with the arbitrators alone. Their function was also honorary and cases were examined free of charge.

At the end of 1977 we had 283 Councils of Arbitration operating in 203 cities with a total of 12 million inhabitants. Seven hundred fifty thousand cases had been settled in a fashion that gave satisfaction to lawyers and litigants alike.

Because they were so successful, we decided in 1977 to further extend the jurisdiction of the Houses of Equity and Councils of Arbitration. These two revolutionary institutions inherited the jurisdiction of the tribunals of Iran's inferior courts.

Was not this utilization—I would dare say enhancement—of popular wisdom *at the roots* a positive revolutionary procedure? I admit that it was a bold experiment. We placed confidence in men of the people and we asked them to judge through their souls and consciences. They made a duty of it and they judged well.

We applied two basic principles: participation and decentralization. We thus achieved a *popular* judicial power. In addition, we demonstrated that there existed a popular elite, both of peasants and of townspeople. This elite is now being decimated but it cannot be annihilated.

The Corps of Literacy, Health and Development, created by Principles 6, 7, 8, and 11 of the White Revolution, played essential roles in the renovation of the villages, improvement of hygiene, and the instruction and intellectual development of the rural population. They were composed of male conscripts and women volunteers.

Since our country throughout this time was growing richer, it became increasingly easy for the government to improve the nation's infrastructure and increase the number of schools, libraries, hospitals, dispensaries, etc. The work of the three Corps was always *in addition* to these efforts. These Corps brought progress to the most isolated regions and focused on "details" which the bureaucratic organizations had overlooked.

The Development and Reconstruction Corps was initially responsible for identifying local problems and then helping to solve them. This required each member to ascertain the geographical, agricultural, economic, social, and cultural conditions of the district. Once determined, it was possible to assess the local problems on the spot. In turn, the Minister of Agriculture was apprised of these evaluations. Next, under the direction of the conscript, a training course in modern agricultural techniques was given. The villagers would sow an experimental field of a thousand square meters with seeds provided by the Ministry. On this land they would learn the best methods of cultivating, harvesting, irrigating, and fertilizing the land, as well as combatting pests. In experimental orchards they learned the correct methods for planting, grafting, pruning, etc. They also learned to improve hygiene, ventilation, and lighting in cowsheds and stables and how to vaccinate their animals.

Among the services rendered in rural areas were: the construction of roads and water supplies; the creation of health service and medical assistance (where the Health Corps was absent); the construction of public baths, schools and libraries; the installation of electricity; the establishment of postal, telegraph and telephone service; the building of public quarters, cooperative stores, centers for professional education and even banks.

The function of the Health Corps was to treat ailments, prevent or halt epidemics, and promote good hygienic conditions. In eight years the number of people in rural areas who benefitted from medical service increased from one million to almost eight million. In the course of these endeavors, they dug wells, installed pumps, purified canals and springs, channeled water, and installed baths.

Their success was so great that in 1974 the Corps was made responsible for all medical and sanitary services in rural districts. Thus the Corps became the Organization of the Health Corps and Centers for Rural Hygiene.

In 1976 this organization had 1,422 clinics and employed 1,240 doctors, with 400 laboratories and numerous dispensaries existing throughout the rural areas. One of the greatest achievements of the Health Corps was a new confidence of the peasants in "official" medicine. Before, the rural populace had frequented "healers"; but by 1978 they would go directly to the Health Corps clinic. This was an outstanding accomplishment in a country where in earlier days a doctor often had to give women patients an injection through a curtain under the surveillance of her father or husband.

Like the other two Corps, the purpose of the Literacy Corps was to supplement the traditional efforts of the government. It did not replace them.

There was in Iran under the Qajars hardly one literate person in a hundred—in a country which had given the world such intellects as al-Farabi, Rhazes, al-Hallaj, Avicenna, the two Ghazzali brothers, Hafiz, Suhrawardi, Omar Khayyam, Firdowsi, Ruzbehan Bagli, and so many others.

Before 1963 less than 24 percent of children between the ages of 6 and 12 went to school in the provinces. The rest remained illiterate. In the cities, 74 percent attended school. Compulsory education was passed into law in 1943 but the law remained unenforced. Thus, on the national level, 85.1 percent of Iranians were illiterate. In 1956, 4 million children were ready for school, but the schools had room for only 1.7 million. More than 2 million young Iranians would have to live as illiterates.

I felt that the solution to this intractable problem lay in the heart of every young Iranian. If we asked qualified conscripts to educate illiterates in the villages without schools, could one imagine that they would refuse? *No!* They agreed, with enthusiasm, and soon gained the respect and esteem of everyone. Many were those who admired our Literacy Corps.

The results were spectacular: the number of pupils in Literacy Corps schools increased by 692 percent in fifteen years. During the first five years alone, 510,000 boys, 128,000 girls, 250,000 men and 12,000 women attended classes organized in the villages.

The Literacy Corps also built and repaired schools, mosques, and public baths, dredged subterranean canals, planted trees, organized sports clubs, and installed letter boxes to enable regular mail delivery.

By 1978 more than 100,000 had served in the Literacy Corps. Many of the conscripts and volunteers became licensed school teachers, while others worked in the village courts of justice. This type of education cost the state, or rather the Iranian community, but one-third of ordinary school costs.

The three Corps were in effect the soldiers of the revolution—versatile, bold and courageous young men and women who never refused a new challenge. Assigned an area, they did all that was possible to improve local living conditions.

To me, the future of the Corps of Literacy and Health rested in telecommunications. Three satellites each with three television channels would be put into fixed orbit. Thus, a medical soldier or nurse confronted with a serious illness in a remote village could seek medical advice from the most eminent specialist in Teheran or elsewhere. This specialist could then explain the required treatment. Such a system would have placed the talent and the experience of the greatest professors and the science of the best doctors at the disposal of the poorest and most isolated Iranians. At the same time, a telecommunication program costing at least 30 billion dollars would have permitted any small Iranian village to communicate automatically with the rest of the world. Here again, I wanted Iran to enter into the age of computerized telecommunications. That was in part the significance of the Great Civilization.

Here is the sum total of our diverse efforts in education for the fifteen-year period 1963-1978:

* * *

Percentage Increase of Students

Nursery	1,350%
Primary School	506%
Middle School	263%
Secondary School	331%
Technical and professional education	1,550%
Schools of the Literacy Corps	692%

The total number of Iranian students increased from 1.5 million in 1963 to more than 10 million in 1978. Credit for this achievement belongs largely to the Literacy Corps, which did more than just instruct. It instilled a thirst for knowledge.

Thus, enrollment in rural primary schools, which in 1963 represented 39.4 percent of the nation's total primary enrollment, rose by 1978 to 52.8 percent, roughly equivalent to the percentage of our rural population. The total number of schools in Iran was to multiply by a factor of 3.24. Finally, the education budget had increased in proportions which I doubt many countries have equalled:

Education Budget

Third Development Plan (1963-67)—45 billion rials
Fourth Development Plan (1968-72)—172 billion rials
Fifth Development Plan (1973-77)—551 billion rials

The budget for the Sixth Plan (1978-82) included 2,500-2,700 billion rials for education. It seems unlikely that this budget will ever be realized. Population trends have indicated that by 1982 we would have had 13.7 million students at school, roughly a 40 percent increase over 1978. What will now happen to these boys and girls?

To educate was fine. However, we needed to improve the quality of teaching and adapt it to the necessities of the modern life of Iran. This concern for improvement was embodied in the 12th Principle of our White Revolution.

Its primary aim was to diversify the materials, methods, and techniques of education in response to the real needs of Iranians of today and tomorrow. This diversification was reflected in the greater emphasis placed on the history of Iran, both modern and ancient—the renaissance of the traditions and folklore of Persian culture and the teaching of Persian language and literature, particularly its lovely poetry. Technical and professional education was enhanced. Classical education, starting from the secondary level, was reformed as well.

We were quick to employ new techniques of teaching (audio-visual, television). Adult education through evening courses and apprenticeships was also provided. The three telecommunication satellites mentioned in connection with the Health Corps were to have made possible a televised education of the highest quality for all our villages.

Free and obligatory education had been announced in principle by my father. Unfortunately, the means were lacking. We had been able to provide free primary education only in the schools of the Literacy Corps. With the adoption of Principle 15, free education for the first eight years of school was established throughout Iran.

Education beyond this was free to all students who agreed to a period of government service after completion of their studies. The term of this service was determined by the time spent in government supported study. Thus, one who completed high school was obligated to four years of government service. Of course, one could free oneself from this obligation by paying back the cost of one's studies, but it seemed to us that requiring the students to serve the state for a few years at the end of their education was more favor than inconvenience, since in this way they were assured of employment and of earning a good livelihood.

In 1978 7.4 million Iranians were enrolled in our public schools. This figure includes nursery, primary, and professional schools as well as the free night school and special training we provided illiterate adults. That year we had 185,000 students of both sexes in our own universities. In addition, about 100,000 pursued college study abroad and of these, 50,000 were enrolled in United States colleges.

We had established eighteen universities and 137 colleges in Iran. Of these, the campuses at Shiraz and Isfahan were designed to stand with the most beautiful in the world. The sites had been carefully chosen and the installations studied in every detail. A third campus had been planned for Hamadan, where instruction was to be carried out in French.

The majority of our students received not only scholarships but pocket money as well. Born at the end of the 50s, they were unaware of the difficulties which had faced their parents and grandparents. They found it quite natural that the best of facilities should be placed at their disposal.

Today I have come to realize that the events of 1978-79 are attributable in part to the fact that I moved too rapidly in opening the doors of the universities, without imposing a more severe preliminary selection. The entrance examinations were too easy. André Malraux used to tell me that, "it is necessary to have ten thousand knights in a country." I believe he was right. Part of my error was my failure to demonstrate to my people that knights can be artisans, workers, and smiths as well as intellectuals and professionals.

The most urgent task was to prepare our young for the multi-faceted, science-oriented world of tomorrow. We wanted them to be supported by solid spiritual and moral training, but to be armed as well with good technical knowledge. Everything possible was done to facilitate the entry of the young into universities.

Many fathers who had never left their villages could not imagine in a dream what their sons were offered: namely, an easy life, nothing to do but study in a big city, often in an agreeable group, with libraries and laboratories at their disposal and prospects of trips to foreign countries.

Some of our students were not prepared to face so many novelties. They lacked the spiritual maturity to confront the apparent ease of their new lives. Sometimes they slid into laziness but most often took to confrontation and disputation. They had received so much without any effort that it appeared natural to them to claim ever more.

Like spoiled children, these students caused so many confrontations that Iranian universities finally sank into anarchy. Today, regrettably, students dictate the academic program since they "vote" at the age of 15. Many disheartened professors have left or are leaving a country, where authority has at the present become null and void. In Teheran alone, of the 2,000 faculty members of the University, 1,200 have asked for early retirement.

If the educational system fails to provide our youth with the intellectual and technical tools necessary in the world of today and tomorrow, and if the teaching of modern sciences falters, Iran will sink back among the fifth rate powers.

I believe that our culture belongs to every Iranian, that it is not the exclusive domain of the privileged. I tried to make it available to all. The Empress was also deeply involved with arts and letters.

The concept that all things belonging to the past were reactionary, anti-progressive and *dépassé* was widespread among Iran's bourgeois city dwellers. The attitude tended to denigrate Iranian culture and caused our people to neglect the works of art bequeathed by the past.

To protect and restore the ancient artistic traditions of our people and culture, the Empress helped expand public libraries, organized contests, exhibitions and festivals, and in general stimulated and encouraged new talent.

Working together, we were able to restore the most beautiful aspects of Persian culture to a place of honor. I have spoken of changes carried out in school programs which brought our classical poetry to eminence. Thanks to television, our old Persian music was saved from neglect, and came to be admired by a great number of people.

At the same time as our traditional culture was being revived, the boldest and the most avant-garde artists met and performed at our festivals and in our modern theaters. The Empress was a crucial force in these endeavors.

Architectural problems were serious, because the tendency, as in many other fields, was to imitate the West. Real estate developers erected modern buildings of a style and scale which were often out of harmony with the countryside and the people of Iran. The Empress intervened many times to persuade builders to restore certain quarters of villages rather than to destroy them in order to completely rebuild. However, as all foreigners who have visited our country know, we also innovated bold new styles with very fine results.

Justice and common sense required that women enjoy the same political rights as men. Hence Principle 5 of the White Revolution reformed the electoral laws and made suffrage in Iran truly universal.

Before our Revolution, Article 10 of the Iranian Electoral Law read: "The following are barred from voting: women; those who are not legally able and are under guardianship; the bankrupt; the insane; beggars and those who earn their livings by dishonorable means; criminals, thieves and other wrong-doers who have violated Islamic laws."

This is the mentality of the so-called revolutionaries who have usurped power in Iran. But we who wanted to place the nation on the path to progress could not relegate our mothers, sisters, wives and daughters to the same category as the insane and the criminal. This is not the concept of the Holy Koran! Women's rights in Islam are considerably greater than is generally known. For example, women always had the right to manage their own fortunes.

We, who are the heirs of a culture and a civilization which had never considered women as inferior beings, believe that in this area we are acting in accordance with the true spirit of our religion and our country's past.

Several thousand years ago, Iranian theology defined two groups of angels, each possessing equal rights. One group consisted of three men, the other of three women. Iran's great religious work of ancient times, the *Din Kard,* specifies that women have the right to manage their fortunes, to represent their husbands at court, to be the guardian of a child disinherited by its father, to become a judge or arbitrator and even, in certain cases, to fulfill the functions of priests.

I have never believed that women were diabolical creatures if they showed their faces or arms, or went swimming, or skied or played basketball. If some women wish to live veiled, then that is their choice, but why deprive half of our youth of the healthy pleasure of sports? Some of our clergy do not understand that to emphasize sports is to improve the health of our people—the most precious possession of any nation.

The use of the chaddor can only inhibit activities that have become commonplace among Iranian women since the White Revolution. Our women have successfully administered public affairs. We have had women ministers and secretaries in the cabinet, an ambassadress, female judges and university professors; women have been elected as heads of municipal councils, deputies and senators. They have also played a vital role in our fight against illiteracy and in the Health Corps.

Today, under the social order of the so-called Islamic Republic, all this is impossible. When half the population is denied education and is forced to live in the past, the whole of society suffers the consequences. Our own prophet Ali said: "Raise your children according to your generation." This return to archaic practices will prevent Iranian women from raising their children for the 21st century!

Health care and social security were two vital fields in which we lagged a good fifty years behind major western countries.

Principle 17 of our White Revolution concerned nationwide Social Security and pensions. Social Security was to guarantee the working population against accident, sickness and incapacity to work. It was designed, moreover, to protect every Iranian through various stages of life. Particular attention was paid to the aged, young married couples and families. Gifted youngsters of both sexes were also put under the Social Security umbrella.

Our Social Security system, in fact, was one of the most progressive in the world, paying pensions in the lower income brackets as high as 100 percent of salaries earned at retirement. Moreover, pensions were increased in direct proportion to the cost of living.

Principle 16 provided free food for needy mothers and new-born children. This law would set the stage for broadly expanded national health care. We fought epidemics, pushed a vaccination program, environmental improvement and better sanitation. Health passes were issued to all citizens, recording vaccinations and other pertinent health data.

I have always believed that the protection of public health is the principal objective of a government. For that reason we created a number of institutions slated for health care.*

The oldest were the Red Lion and Sun, which dated from my father's reign, the Imperial Organization for Social Services, and the Organization for the Protection of Mothers and the Newly Born. In addition to providing health care and hygiene for handicapped and retarded youth, they taught handicrafts and gave vocational training. They trained nurses and social workers. They surveyed the condition of working women and youth in factories and where possible proposed legal remedies to ameliorate adverse conditions.

The Empress was preoccupied with many of these institutions, putting her heart and soul into them. I shall cite several examples.

Although today the cure of leprosy has become commonplace, the re-integration of cured lepers into society continues to pose great difficulties, for the fear of lepers is an ingrained one. Our lepers, once cured, were still ostracized. To solve this dilemma, the Empress offered a new approach: a perfect model village was built for the cured lepers. It caused such envy and curiosity in the surrounding areas that people flocked to

---

*Appendix II contains a list of other national health organizations

see it. When the Empress herself visited the village she was overwhelmed by the affection showered upon her.

In the course of her efforts to improve and modernize the condition of women, the Empress encountered difficulties born of deeply rooted manners and customs. She always found conciliatory solutions. For example, in Baluchistan where the girls were not allowed to speak to men, the girl volunteers of the three Corps were sent to assist them, while the conscripts looked after the men.

Yet, despite the opposition of conservative forces, many prejudices were gradually surmounted. In most regions not only did school classes become mixed, not only were women treated by male doctors, but one could see nurses arriving on motorcycles to attend to male patients; one could also see female medical students and social workers on motorcycles. This indeed was a great revolution!

It was the Empress who encouraged the Organization for the Protection of Children, which reviewed with the help of magistrates, current legislation concerning minors. This organization was particularly active in hospitals, children's clinics and maternity wards and in teaching the care of infants and family planning.

All the social organizations which functioned under the aegis of the Empress assisted and supplemented the work of official government institutions. In fact, their popular success was not surprising, for volunteers always put their hearts into their efforts.

My major charitable endeavor was the Pahlavi Foundation, created in 1958 and charged with social and cultural responsibilities. In 1961 its administrative structure was established and I officially endowed it with sufficient funding to meet its goals. This endowment consisted of personal holdings: land, real estate, hotels, and shares of various enterprises such as the Omran Bank, Melli Insurance, factories, etc. In addition in New York an independent branch of the Foundation was set up in New York City where it purchased a piece of real estate. The anticipated revenues from the rentals of this property would be sufficient to support the works of the New York adjunct of the Foundation.

Since my position as president was honorary, a director and an administrative council managed the foundation. They were controlled and supervised by a special commission comprised of the prime minister, the Presidents of the Senate and Chamber of Deputies, the president of the Supreme Court, and four individuals respected for their spiritual and moral values. Each year this commission published a report on the activities of the Foundation, which detailed its administrative and financial endeavors.

The Foundation concentrated most of its activities in the cultural area and university students were its main beneficiaries. By 1977, 13,000 students from deserving families had received scholarships that enabled them to complete their studies at home or abroad. Although we had many State scholarship students, the Pahlavi scholars were considered an elite group.

The Institute for the Translation and Publication of books became an important branch of the Foundation. In 1977 this Institute had published more than 500 sociological, religious, historical or literary works of international cultural interest, as well as many masterpieces from our own undiscovered literature. Annually, I would reward the winners of the "Best Book Contest" to authors and translators who had been selected by a panel of university professors. Also prizes were awarded to successful primary and secondary school students from poor families.

The maintenance and repair of numerous mosques and the heating and lighting of many theological seminaries, especially those in Qum, were paid for by the Foundation, which subsidized financially needy religious publications as well. Certain social work activities of the Empress also benefited from the Foundation.

In 1977, when the rents for 3-4 room apartments in Teheran had skyrocketed to between $700-$800 per month, the Foundation undertook the construction of low-rent housing. We hoped this endeavor would force speculators to lower their prices. In its first stage, 6,000 low-income apartments were built by the foundation. Others were to follow, as brick and cement production permitted.

The creation of the Pahlavi Foundation was for me an act of a religious nature. For the Western reader, I must explain that such donations in Iran are irrevocable and inalienable. Thus, those responsible for the management of a foundation must use the funds at their disposal only for the purposes specified by the donor. While I was in Iran, this principle was never violated. Today, I do not know if this principle is still honored by the new regime. I do not know if the foundation is still financing studies of young Iranians abroad, to cite but one example.

Due to the confusion in the Western press, I feel obliged to state clearly that I never profited in any manner from the Pahlavi Foundation. Moreover, in November 1978 I donated all my Iranian holdings to the Foundation. I acted out of conviction and therefore, have no reasons for regrets.

Iran was a developing nation, with a population of 27 million in 1968, 36 million in 1978 and probably 50 million in 1990. This meant that each year we had literally a million new mouths to feed, new housing requirements, and a million new jobs to fill. These issues were further complicated by a massive migration from rural to urban areas.

In 1956 Teheran had a population of 1.7 million; in 1978 it was 4.5 million. Other major towns showed similar increases:

	1956	1976
Isfahan	255,000	1,000,000
Tabriz	300,000	900,000
Meshed	250,000	950,000
Shiraz	171,000	750,000

In Iran as elsewhere this migration posed problems of extreme complexity.

First and foremost was housing for workers which required complex urban reforms. We had to rebuild and convert many residential quarters. This entailed especially strict control of the plans of most real estate owners and builders, who were too often concerned only with profits. Controls were placed on the rapidly rising land prices, and various forms of land speculation were penalized. This was Principle 18 of our White Revolution, adopted in 1977. At the same time, the government embarked on a program of low-cost public housing that utilized private contractors and resources of existing and newly created financial institutions like savings and commercial banks and government-guaranteed loans. Prospective home or apartment buyers were extended low-cost, long-term loans.

By the end of 1977 some 31,000 government-sponsored housing units had been completed at a cost of 14.4 billion rials ($200 million). Another 40,000 units were under construction. Plans also called for the construction of worker housing near factories and plants.

Facilities for use by young people were on our drawing boards, more than 2,000 of them, and included schools, universities, hospitals, sports complexes, hotels and holiday camps.

Unfortunately, since our infrastructure was weak, our housing construction could not keep pace with the rising population. We were still too dependent on imported materials for building; our port capacities were still inadequate. Thus, ships often waited six months or more to unload their cargoes. Our lack of an adequate highway system to transport unloaded materials inland further exacerbated our housing shortages.

Another problem stemmed from the general insufficiency of personnel. Although Iran had no unemployment when I left and we employed over one million foreigners and were implementing extensive training programs for Iranians, we still suffered severe skilled labor shortages. The training of our labor force could not keep pace with the advances of our country.

These weaknesses in our infrastructure played a role in the deterioration of our social and political climate. They contributed to our inflation problem, which we constantly sought to control. I believe these bottlenecks were temporary and that by 1982 Iran would have had the necessary infrastructure to meet its needs.

Administrative reform of our bureaucracy constituted the 12th Principle of our White Revolution, and was indeed essential. We knew we were attacking a hydra-headed monster, which made its lair in a mountain of paper.

Ideally, to administer the government is to serve one's country. To achieve, or even to approach this ideal, the individual official must be imbued with concern for the common good. Our task was to impose a moral and intellectual reform in circles heretofore hostile to any change. Reform of our administration became more urgent as our population increased, our country expanded, and our bureaucracy decentralized.

All these factors had contributed to the multiplication of public services and the creation of new programs.

To attack this evil at its roots required Administrative reorganization which could only occur if the attitudes of the workers changed. To better achieve this end, we made the administrative revolution a part of our educational revolution, for its goal was to help Iranians acquire the needed intellectual and moral maturity.

Our three Corps of Literacy, Health and Development had been conceived in part to minimize bureaucratic interference and to create a new mentality in the country. I hoped that our educational system, revitalized by the Ramsar Charter,* would impart this new philosophy to Iran's youth. The nation would then see its young men and women step forward as trustworthy public servants with open minds toward the modern world.

While our educational revolution offered hope for the future, the need for improvement was immediate. A Council for Administrative Reform was assigned to each governmental ministry and was charged with implementing reforms. These improvements included modernization, decentralization and simplification of bureaucratic procedures and the use of computers where possible. These committees did their best, and their work was evidenced by many advances in procedures and methods.

On March 4, 1974 the Resurgence Party was formed. I believed that representatives of all social levels and all opinions could be gathered together in one party. I thought that through eliminating an opposition party, I could solicit the aid of all capable political personalities without concern for party politics. For the future I saw this organization as a great political and ideological school, able to engender the civic spirit necessary for administrative reform.

The Resurgence Party would foster the convergence of many essential goals which we were then pursuing through government channels. However, experience was to show that the creation of this party was an error. President Sadat had to suppress the single party in Egypt and return to pluralism. I believe that he was right for the Resurgence Party did not succeed in achieving its objectives—it did not become the conduit of ideas, needs and wishes between the nation and the government.

During the years 1975 through 1978, the stubborn strength of bureaucratic resistance became obvious. The monster changed form, sometimes it took on a progressive appearance, sometimes an honorable traditionalist dye, but it always resisted reform.

In 1959 we had created the Organization of Imperial Inspection. It was a modern version of what the ancient Persians had called "the eyes and ears of the King" and operated much as does the Swedish ombuds-

*Concern for improvement was expressed in August 1968 in a document called "The Charter for Educational Revolution" which was drawn up at a teaching congress held at Ramsar.

man. It consisted of a group of people of proven integrity, who were directly responsible to me. They travelled throughout the country incognito to observe what was or was not functioning. Any Iranian could apply to this body to complain of injustice, bureaucratic delays, or irregularities in the use of public funds.

Lies, extortion, and embezzlement had for so long been the practice that they had become literally endemic to our bureaucracy. In setting up the Organization of Imperial Inspection, I hoped to avoid these abuses by anticipating them, and at least for some officials, the very existence of the Imperial Inspectorate served in lieu of a conscience.

However, in 1961 our Prime Minister, Ali Amini, dissolved the Organization of Imperial Inspection on the grounds of economy, although its yearly budget was only $300,000. This decision was a major mistake, not soon enough rectified. On November 7, 1976, the institution was revived under the name of the Imperial Inspection Commission and Hossein Fardoust was appointed as its director. It was made up of representatives from administrative bodies, from the Resurgence Party—that was the time of our one-party system—the Chambers of Commerce, Industry and Mining, and finally from the mass media. The Commission's function was to study the programs of ministries, monitor their operation and correct serious organizational problems.

It was a modernized service for the inspection of the affairs of the country. This method of self evaluation seemed to me to be surer and also more impartial than that of the "loyal opposition" on which Western nations must rely. Opponents rarely base their criticism on objective observations. Unfortunately, like many of our later provisions, it hardly had time to bear fruit.

While actively attempting administrative reform, we were at the same time occupied with decentralization, which of necessity multiplies the bureaucratic cadre. We were fighting against the clock, for with a vastly enlarged bureaucracy, failure in reform would have the gravest consequences.

Today under the so-called Islamic Republic, the caliber of the government staff is of much less importance, for little remains to administer; and as the nation's wealth diminishes, so does the profit from graft.

There were two objectives in the White Revolution whose realization would affect speculators and racketeers. They aimed at fighting inflation and speculation (Principle 14) and corruption (Principle 19). These endeavors I knew would set certain elements of the population against me: affluent and powerful people who cared little about the methods employed in obtaining their wealth.

The 14th Principle was put into effect in August, 1975. At that time we were suffering an inflation of 20% which endangered our economy and social equilibrium. Existing laws could not control rising prices. From 1975 to 1977 our fight against inflation seemed to be succeeding. The cost of living index was down 5% and the growth of the money supply had been curbed without hampering economic expansion. But in 1977, consumer prices began to rise again. Price guidelines were not respected. Appeals to major firms to hold the line were ignored.

We then made a major mistake—we asked student volunteers to work as price controllers. Their excessive zeal, their occasional threats, and their ignorance of commercial realities alienated many retailers. Some of these young controllers were probably simply set on sabotaging our government.

As a result, retailers often found themselves caught between wholesalers who increasingly demanded higher prices and intransigent hotheaded young people who required small shopkeepers to sell at a loss. Some merchants in the bazaars felt that they were being unjustly wronged and strongly opposed the 14th Principle.

In order to punish crimes against this principle, special tribunals were instituted which passed judgment without appeal. During August and September of 1977, 8,000 people were tried for price control violations. We made every effort to mete out punishment at the top. Owners of factories and large chain stores were heavily fined; some were imprisoned and others' licenses were revoked.

Sanctions were imposed on multi-national foreign companies, union officials, deputy prefects, mayors, and highly placed civil servants. Tons of merchandise stored for speculative purposes were confiscated and sold to consumers at fixed prices. At the same time, new laws were promulgated to regulate the market. Nevertheless, prices continued to rise.

The 19th Principle was designed to protect our society against corruption, especially influence peddling. Henceforth, all government officials—ministers, governors of provinces, mayors, etc.—were required to disclose their net worth. Stocks had to be exchanged for Treasury Bonds

(13 percent interest, tax exempt) or deposited and managed by banks, investment companies or similar organizations for the duration of any official's term of office.

This Principle was not only part of my government's fight against corruption but also a pillar of Iran's moral and social order. Politics based on the selling of favors and nepotism had cost the country dearly and had to be ended. Employment in the government or in the provinces now was only open to those interested in working and serving the nation honestly. At the same time, it was equally important for highly placed officials to be well paid since low bureaucratic salaries are often a cause of corruption.

This is my understanding of democracy. Our White Revolution assured everyone of the same economic and social privileges, with the same responsibilities. Therefore, these measures were not at all demagogic; they were taken for the protection of the public.

Systematic application of the 19th Principle should have given high bureaucrats the prestige necessary for them to set an example for others. In the long run, we would have perhaps succeeded in ending corruption.

Although corruption exists everywhere, we went to great lengths to free our government from it. On at least two occasions, I personally intervened and told foreign suppliers that we would not tolerate their practices.

One involved a telecommunications contract with a multi-national concern. At issue were $12 million in bribes to unauthorized Iranians. When we uncovered this scandal, we insisted that the foreign company repay this $12 million to the Iranian government.

A second incident involved an order of 80 F-14 airplanes from Grumman Corp. When we learned that Grumman planned to pay $28 million to two uninvolved Iranian middlemen, we insisted that the company pay that amount to the government. They did so in the form of spare parts.

Our attitude was the same in our negotiations with French firms engaged to build our subway system. At the outset, we said "No commissions," and they agreed.

In mid-1978, I signed a decree regarding "the ethical conduct of the Imperial Family." By the terms of this fiat all complaints against my family were to be referred to a special commission composed of three judges chosen by the Minister of Justice. This commission did not preclude anyone from bringing complaints regarding members of my family before ordinary courts. Many people warned me that I had thus provided my opposition with a rod to beat me.

Our domestic politics was based on participation, decentralization, and democratization. Our White Revolution breathed life into these principles.

The Houses of Equity, village councils, mayors, governors, and provincial councils with extended powers were instruments of political interaction. The participation of labor in management and profit-sharing produced similar results in our economic structure.

State centralization would continue, of course, for the armed forces, the conduct of foreign affairs, finance, the state and local police, and public education.

I viewed central control of public education as one means of insuring national unity. Iran is a mosaic of many tribes and nationalities with different cultures and traditions. Teaching the Persian language throughout our country fostered a common bond among all.

The love of one's village, the city or province of one's birth, freed from the yoke of centralism, was not at all incompatible with love for the Iranian nation. On the contrary, it increased this love and devotion.

Popular participation was compatible and often intermingled with decentralization, which I emphasized during the last years and which I had hoped to expand.

These concepts required a radical reform of the administration. This is why we focused our efforts on training good civil servants who would be patriots, honest, devoted, and capable of taking initiative. By 1982, three million more people would join our work force. This added force would be comprised of engineers, doctors, technicians and other professionals graduating from our institutions of higher learning.

The advent of democratization in the sense that I understand it is very difficult without participation or decentralization. I realized Iran's need for democracy early in my reign.

One day my father told me that he hoped to leave me an empire "whose solid institutions made it capable of existing and practically governing itself by itself." I was then very young and was hurt by this proposition—which I interpreted to mean a lack of confidence in me. I thought that Reza Shah was expressing doubt about my capacity to govern.

Then came his abdication and the occupation. During these tribulations I realized that although one may inherit a crown, power can only be earned. Especially in a constitutional monarchy such as ours, power must be obtained with the help of the people. Thus, its only valid use is on behalf of the people. Later, while fighting against Iran's oligarchy, I saw the creation of truly democratic institutions as an absolute necessity for Iran.

Democratization at all levels of Iranian life can flourish only under the aegis of a constitutional monarchy. Iran had always been and remains an *empire,* that is, an assemblage of people whose ethnic character, language, manners, and even religious beliefs are different. (Muslims constitute an imposing majority.) Hence, the necessity of a sovereign who would bring about unity from above in order to realize a true imperial democracy.

The union of these two words should not be surprising. According to Iran's Constitution, be it that of 1906 or 1950, although the Emperor submits his projects for acceptance by the government, he nevertheless remains a constitutional monarch. He reigns but does not rule.

Imperial democracy is the gathering of all our ethnic groups under the same democratic standard within our frontiers. It is the union of all our social classes in the struggle for true progress.

10

Foreign Policy

None of the goals of our White Revolution could have been achieved if we had not been able to maintain peace with our neighbors in a strategic region of the world of which Iran is the focal point.

My essential objective in foreign policy was therefore to have good neighborly relations with all countries of the region.

Although we had no belligerent intentions toward others we made it known that Iran would resist aggression from whatever quarter.

Once our position was well understood, we were able to satisfactorily negotiate a number of issues with the Soviet Union. We reached agreement on matters concerning our common frontiers. We divided the waters of the Arax River according to international law and constructed (on a 50/50 basis) a dam on this river which produced electricity and permitted irrigation of vast agricultural areas. We were working on similar 50/50 projects with the Russians to provide additional irrigation and electricity from the same river. Our common production of electricity would have reached one million KWH in the eighties.

The considerable volume of trade with the Soviet Union made it one of our principal partners. We furnished the Soviets with gas while they built an important steel mill for us in Isfahan. The Americans, under

Eisenhower, had been undecided on undertaking this project. The Russians also helped us to prospect and discover iron and coal mines north of the desert (south of Khorasan) and near Kerman. The volume of Western merchandise shipped through Russia to Iran reached enormous proportions and became an important element in our trade relations.

Quite naturally, I had many occasions to meet with Leonid Brezhnev in the Soviet Union and Iran. Ideological differences aside, I sincerely admire Mr. Brezhnev. He is a superb diplomat who has brought his country to the apogee of power we see today. The Soviet Union is the first nuclear power of the world and soon will be the first naval power. As for ground and airborne forces, its superiority is so great that it defies comparison.

I must add that we purchased large supplies of military equipment from the Russians as well as the Czechs. I was always cordially received in Czechoslavakia and the other socialist countries of Eastern Europe, and made great friends with leaders of several of these nations.

Yugoslavia is the only country, along with Iran, to have stood up to Josef Stalin under difficult if not anguishing circumstances. It was not easy to unify various ethnic groups and modernize a country like Yugoslavia. One must understand that Marshall Tito accomplished an extraordinary task. May God make his successors show themselves to be as capable as he was.

President Ceausescu of Rumania impressed me with his intransigent patriotism and his fierce, independent will. He is a strong leader capable of insuring his nation's independence. Through our meetings and conversations, we became good friends. This relationship deepened as our mutual trade endeavors grew. His loyal friendship has been sincerely appreciated during these difficult times.

Since my father's time Turkey and Iran have been faithful friends. For Iran, the prosperity and greatness of Turkey were of fundamental importance. Today I fervently pray for the happiness of this valiant people.

Our alliance was cemented by the 1956 Baghdad Pact. My meeting with Khrushchev took place shortly afterward. He was not pleased and welcomed me by saying "This pact is aggressive, directed against us!"

I pointed out to him that in political and journalistic circles there was talk of a line of defense passing through the Zagros mountains. And I asked,

"Where are these mountains, in Russia or in Iran?"

"In Iran."

"It is then surely a defensive pact," I responded.

Kruschev added, still in a truculent vein, "Don't make me laugh with your pacts. . . ! You know perfectly well that we could flatten England with seven atom bombs and Turkey with twelve!"

He was not a man for conversation—sometimes gruff, always obstinate. But his peasant upbringing, which made him alternately good-natured and cunning, also made him likeable. Together we agreed on a policy of neighborliness which good sense dictated and we held resolutely to it.

Later Khrushchev declared that the Baghdad Pact would break up like a soap bubble. Twenty-five years later one has to admit that he was right.

During the Algiers oil conference in 1975, I spoke at length with Saddam Hussein, the president of Iraq. We agreed to bury our differences and succeeded in ending the misunderstandings which colonialist influences had maintained between us.

President Hussein agreed to negotiate the question of the River Chatt-El-Arab according to international law. As in the case of the Arax River, the waters were divided midway between Iraq and Iran. All our land disputes were also settled.

In principle, I told President Hussein that the happiness and prosperity of Iraq were important to the security of Iran.

This same principle led us to aid Afghanistan when it was facing certain economic difficulties. Subsequently, a change of government and of political orientation took place in Afghanistan. The Western powers were not in the least concerned.

We recognized the new Afghan regime and continued our economic aid. I was puzzled by the West's indifference and concerned about the implications for Iran. Was it a question of a policy change of the superpowers in this region?

I was the first head of state to visit Pakistan when it gained independence. We were always faithful allies of this new republic which we aided economically and militarily. We worked for the establishment of peaceful and lasting relations between Islamic Pakistan and India. An Indo-

Pakistani confrontation always appeared to me to be terribly dangerous.

This is why I wanted to take advantage of the presence in Persepolis of the then president of Pakistan, General Yahya Khan, on the occasion of the 2,500th anniversary of the Persian Empire. I hoped to arrange a meeting between him and the President of the USSR, Podgorny, and thus to help avert the impending conflict between India and Pakistan over Bangladesh.

We also had friendly relations with our neighbors on the other side of the Persian Gulf—Kuwait, the Emirates, and especially Saudi Arabia.

I had traveled on several occasions to Saudi Arabia, a country whose integrity and independence are sacred for all Muslims. Twice I had the great joy of making the supreme pilgrimage. As a faithful Muslim and Defender of the Faith, I hope that Saudi Arabia will always remain the guardian of these holy places, Mecca and Medina, where millions of pilgrims travel every year on the path to God.

History has recorded the stature of Ibn Saud, founder of Saudi Arabia. He was wise and brave and an excellent administrator. When one considers the fatal events for which Iran is now the theater, one cannot but rejoice at seeing Saudi Arabia still free and independent. One can only pray to God that it remains so.

In 1973, at the request of the Sultanate of Oman, I provided this state with military aid. Oman was then threatened by the Zofaris, who were supported by Southern Yemen, the communists, and the Chinese. Our troops in Oman intervened in a vigorous way until the Sultan, who is my friend, succeeded in dominating the situation.

China retired from this conflict after establishing diplomatic relations with Iran. China was not playing a double game; at the time of President Hua Kuo-Feng's visit to Teheran in August 1978, the Iranian crisis was reaching its peak. I was impressed by the Chinese leader's integrity and very sound knowledge of international politics. After talking to him, I realized China was among the few nations interested in a strong Iran.

I felt that a policy of solidarity was necessary among the Persian Gulf countries, who were faced with increasing dangers.

Similarly, all of the countries vitally interested in the Indian Ocean—Iran, Pakistan, India, Sri Lanka, Bengladesh, Burma, Malaysia, Thailand,

Singapore, Indonesia, Australia and New Zealand and all the countries of East Africa—should combine for their collective security. A Southeast Asian pact was supposed to provide this protection but it was practically dead.

I deeply felt that the creation of a zone of peace and stabiiity around the Indian Ocean would serve the cause of world peace. It could have succeeded. However, would it have been tolerated? It would have precluded both Russian and American intervention. Could the Soviet Union and the U.S. admit that their armed presence in the Indian Ocean was not necessary?

During a visit to Australia in 1974, I proposed, the creation of a common market for countries bordering on the Indian Ocean. I made the same proposal in Singapore and in India. This concept was everywhere well received.

Under my plan, after studying the possibilities and needs of the member countries, a program of exchange and mutual assistance would be put into action. I had declared, for example, that Iran would be ready to contribute to the industrialization of India, and the development of its mines and agricultural lands.

Without waiting for the realization of the common market, we furnished economic aid to the Sudan, Somalia, and even to Senegal and other countries in West Africa and in the interior of Black Africa. I intervened with leaders of South Africa in an attempt to find an acceptable solution for the Namibian affair. I also met with all Black Rhodesian leaders in order to encourage an equitable and peaceful solution there. This move for peace brought me at that time the thanks of the Anglo-Americans.

Iran, which is only separated from Africa by the Arabian Peninsula, the Red Sea, and the Indian Ocean, was concerned to see communist penetration into Africa along three axes: The first, going from Libya toward Chad, the Sudan, and Somalia, is the Mediterranean–Red Sea–Indian Ocean axis; the second aims to link the Mediterranean to the Atlantic by land; and the third cuts Africa in two from Angola to Mozambique. The axes of Communist penetration in Africa are real dividing lines. Both the longitudinal and transverse axes sever the African continent. This penetration is a vast strategic movement which threatens to destabilize the whole of Africa. Tomorrow what is called

Black Africa could become Red Africa. (In an effort to thwart such actions, I had dreamed of contributing financially to a modern railway line linking the east and west coasts of Africa.)

It was always with great pleasure that I conversed with the emperor of Ethiopia, Haile Selassie, who displayed great patriotic force in resisting the Italians in the mid-thirties. Our conversations were frank and animated and I sometimes allowed myself to suggest certain reforms to him.

I was a young student when I heard him defend his country without success before the high tribunal of the League of Nations in Geneva. The League was powerless in those days, as is the United Nations in our times. What has happened to Ethiopia today?

We were envisaging giving increased aid to the Ivory Coast presided over by Houphouet-Boigny and to Gabon and Senegal.

Especially strong bonds linked me with President Senghor of Senegal, who influenced the development of my African policy. A diplomat of international prestige and a remarkable administrator, Leopold Senghor is a master of the French language and a true poet. We spoke at length concerning the doctrine of "negritude" which is truly a spiritual synthesis. I empathize with this doctrine, for throughout my life, my Persian roots have been an integral part of me.

Egypt, Jordan, and Morocco happily are in a stable condition thanks to three exceptional men, President Sadat, King Hussein, and King Hassan II.

We must not forget that having succeeded Nasser, Anwar al-Sadat found himself at the head of a country which was not only crushed but humiliated. In Egypt, public opinion had been led astray by deceptive slogans. Sadat took up the fight again and thanks to Soviet arms, gained a first victory. However, he felt the cost of this victory was excessive and it was in order to preserve peace that he thanked the Soviet advisors and established a policy of independence which was of benefit only to the Egyptian people.

To affect such a reversal of policy, one must be endowed with a great political sense as well as great courage. Sadat has already entered into history as one of the most authentic political geniuses that Egypt has known.

I shall never forget with what generosity he welcomed me under dramatic circumstances. It is with fervor that I pray for this great Egyptian and his people.

As for King Hussein of Jordan, I can never praise him enough. To me, he is not only a friend but a brother. He is a strong, good-hearted man in whom great courage unites with a deep love for his country. In numerous instances, Jordan's Hussein has known how to face adversity, and he has done so with resolution. Jordan's strategic position has been independently preserved through King Hussein's political wisdom and decisive spirit. I remember an incident which is illustrative of his valor. A coup d'état, fomented by Gamal Abdel Nasser and led by a Jordanian general, took place in Jordan. There was an uprising in one of the garrisons. King Hussein went *alone* into the insurgent barracks and addressed the troops firmly and reasonably. When he finished speaking, the soldiers cheered and threw themselves at his feet.

As a crown prince my friend Hassan II proved his patriotism. Certainly he must possess the *baraka* to have been able to escape different assassination attempts and to have succeeded in his famous Green March into the middle of the recovered Sahara.

He is a sovereign with a rare intellectual elegance. At once descendant of the Holy Prophet and doctor of law from the University of Bordeaux, he is a perfect incarnation of two cultures, the Koranic and the European.

It is superfluous to add that I pray for him and his faithful people. Words fail me to express here my thanks for the attitude he displayed toward me and my family after the sinister events of January 1979. For his part, it was a challenge to all those who have forgotten the very exalted lessons of the Holy Prophet.

As for our relations with Western countries, Iran placed itself ideologically squarely in the camp of the Western democracies. My country has for many years enjoyed excellent relations with France, which has never shown any imperialist tendencies toward us and his contributed much to our culture and to our economic development. It was as a very young sovereign that I first met General Charles De Gaulle. I was immediately captivated by his extraordinary personality. In listening to him speak of France, I heard echoes of the hopes and dreams which I nurtured for my own country. He had an eloquence that made his faith in the future of his country contagious.

Naturally we were to meet many times either in France or in Iran.

Each time our bonds of friendship were strengthened. These ties were furthered by our ongoing correspondence. Upon his death, I attended the funeral services at Notre Dame and was later received at Colombey by Madame De Gaulle. I was deeply touched by this attention to me during those painful hours.

This ardent patriot was a guide for me as a sovereign. As the measure of his greatness, one has only to compare the conditions of France in 1956 with its conditions at the time he retired from public office.

Our relationship with France was exceptionally strong. However, our economic exchange with the other countries of the OECD, in particular the U.S., was considerable and constant. In addition, we had recently increased our commercial relations with other countries in the Americas.

I have stated clearly that our foreign policy served only one country, Iran. But it was equally clear to us that our own interests were best served when our immediate neighbors were at peace. That is why we always practiced a good neighbor policy and, to the extent of our means, a policy of mutual assistance. This is also why we maintained a just balance in our relations with the West, the U.S.S.R., eastern European countries, and communist China.

The profound and genuine solidarity of all the peoples on earth is not a fantasy to me. It is a reality which, in my opinion, should dominate the foreign policy of *all* nations without exception. I have always aimed with all my country's might toward the achievement of this ideal.

One needs only a glance at a map of the world to realize that of the 150 countries of the earth only 28 are considered democracies in the West's eyes. The common features among all these countries, whether they are predominantly industrial or agricultural, are a prosperous economy and high standards of living.

Outside of this "club of the privileged," the Indian sub-continent, for example, is ruled by governments which are theoretically democratic. But they have done little to remedy the illiteracy of their people, to change poor health care, and to curb civil strife. They refuse to modernize. Their misery stems from a weak economy.

We are touching here on the heart of one of the gravest dilemmas of our epoch. It weighs on all countries which find themselves outside the "club of the privileged." The question is to evolve or not evolve, to remain a docile member of the Third World or to attempt to cross the threshhold and enter into modern civilization.

These countries expose themselves to enormous, if not insurmountable, difficulties. They often have only limited means at their disposal, and almost always lack experience and qualified professionals. They must compete on the world market and vie with intransigent industrialized countries. The privileged have never had to cope with such problems during their evolution. They did not encounter fearsome competitors and could therefore peacefully prepare for democracy. They built solid economies based on their scientific and technological capability. Today's developing countries are not in this enviable position.

It seems that in our epoch no country can pretend to political independence if it lacks a solid economic structure. This is a condition *sine qua non.* For today it is economic power that guarantees freedom and sovereignty for a nation, and furnishes it with the conditions for a true democracy.

Thus, in 1973, I proposed that the twelve industrialized countries join the twelve members of OPEC in creating an International Fund for Aid, each contributing 150 million dollars to it. The council of this Fund would include, besides the 24 founding nations, twelve representatives from Third World nations. The members together would study projects submitted by the developing countries. These plans would aim towards the gradual economic independence of the aided countries.

The World Bank and the International Monetary Fund were to serve as advisors and provide facilities for exchange and financing, agreeing to loans on the basis of 20 years at 2.5 percent a year. Robert McNamara and the president of the International Monetary Fund favored the project.

This program provided a framework in which an international bank for development would aid any Third World country which was in difficulty. This organization would have to be absolutely neutral, independent, politically free from obligation, and open to everyone.

The number of OPEC countries has grown and my earlier proposal should be financially increased. The rises in the price of oil should also be taken into account.

My initial proposal on contributions would have produced three billion dollars. It would be fitting today to collect twenty billion dollars.

The Fund would have played the role of an international cooperative, or better yet the role of an economic United Nations with executive power.

These proposals for international economic cooperation had been made in the framework of a tentative global solution for the problems of energy and as such were taken up in an integral fashion in the article in *Le Monde Diplomatique* already cited.*

Without doubt this project was bold, but it was not chimerical. It made a direct appeal to international solidarity and could have constituted an element of politico-economic stabilization of great efficacy.

I had many conversations with Valéry Giscard d'Estaing, the president of the French Republic, concerning this conference. Our views were in absolute agreement. We agreed that the great politico-economic problems, and particularly those of energy, had to be reconsidered in their totality on a world-wide scale so that international solutions could be found for them. World peace can only be gained at such a price.

I am happy to see that a similar program is finally being given serious attention under UN auspices by the Brandt Commission. This endeavor is long overdue and I pray that Mr. Brandt's efforts will meet with success.

I should not end this chapter without a few words about our armament policies. I have often repeated that Iran harbored no expansionist notions. We had no wish to impose our political, social, or economic concepts on anyone. Our actions in the United Nations were always in the interests of moderation, conciliation, and peace.

However, our policy of strict independence made military strength a necessity. This need had been graphically illustrated throughout Iran's ancient and modern history. When our armed forces were weak, our nation was overrun. When we were strong, our nation was saved from foreign invasion. Often military might alone had been our sole guarantee of survival.

My father, Reza Shah, was keenly aware of this and of the necessity for national armed forces. He knew that to control the rebellious tribal chieftains in the outlying provinces a strong, centrally controlled army was needed. Without domestic peace, Iran could never survive, much less hope to modernize and industrialize.

In 1920 my father took the command of the Persian Cossacks out of the hands of the Russians and began to build our modern military forces. Reza Shah focused most of his attentions on shoring up our domestic

---

*See page 99

security. At that time "Britannia ruled the waves," and thereby protected our nation from foreign aggressors. In the late forties and early fifties, the U.S. under President Truman bolstered our defense system through their Mutual Security Program. On July 25, 1949, President Truman in a special Message to Congress stated: "In Iran the use of surpluses of U.S. military equipment has aided in improving the defensive effectiveness of the Iranian Army.... It is now necessary to provide certain additional items... to strengthen the ability of Iran to defend its independence." In all our discussions I always found Truman to be a straightforward, honest statesman.

Under President Eisenhower, limited military aid was continued through the Mutual Security Program. And in the early sixties, President Kennedy, too, acknowledged the strategic importance of Iran to the West. On a visit to the U.S. in April 1962, Kennedy stated that he considered me to be "... a vital force in maintaining the independence of [my] country.... So when we welcome the Shah here we welcome a friend and a very valiant fighter...." Later during that visit he reaffirmed our bilateral agreement concerning the maintenance of independence and territorial integrity in Iran. We also agreed on the necessity for collective security arrangements.

However, in January 1968, Great Britain announced that it was withdrawing its troops from the Persian Gulf. Three months earlier Mr. Goronwy Roberts, sent by the British Foreign Office, had assured Iran that the British had no intention of leaving the Gulf in the foreseeable future. Their about-face took me by surprise and I can only assume that their prospective entry into the Common Market prompted this reversal. Shortly after, President Nixon declared that the United States would no longer maintain its role as the "world's policeman." Thus, our security could be assured only through our own efforts.

That is why in 1971, on the eve of the British departure, we occupied the islands of Tomb and Abu Musa. In Bahrain, where only one-sixth of the population was Iranian, we agreed to self-determination. Bahrain opted for independence.

By that time Egypt's Nasser had already succeeded in fomenting dissension in the region, and Libya's Qadaffi and the PLO's Arafat continued these incendiary activities. I knew then that as Iran continued to grow and prosper, we would become an increasingly attractive prize for foreign predators of every ilk.

All these circumstances prevented Iran from remaining complacent. The security of our borders required constant vigilance, not only along the Gulf coastline but also to the East, where we faced possible incursions. Afghanistan, Pakistan, and India have all been subject to domestic and foreign strife, quite apart from the sorties of our neighbor the Soviet Union.

Our lifeline was and is the Persian Gulf. We have no oil pipeline to the Mediterranean as do Iraq and Saudi Arabia. The stability of the Gulf of Oman and the Indian Ocean were also of vital concern. Defense of the Straits of Hormuz required that the nations on the Arab side remain our friends. Our forces had to be strong enough to prevent these friendly but poorly-armed governments from being overthrown. Guerilla groups could be deterred only if they knew that Iran was prepared to move rapidly and forcefully to protect these nations.

Outside the Persian Gulf, the sea lanes through the Gulf of Oman, the Arabian Sea, and the Indian Ocean were vulnerable to submarine attack. This aspect of our defense required a substantial investment in our naval capabilities.

Many times I have voiced my firm intention to avoid the use and even the possession of nuclear armaments. Our conventionally armed forces would have been among the finest in the world by 1982. These forces would not only have safeguarded our interests in the Persian Gulf but would have preserved the stability and peace of the Indian Ocean as well.

How much armament is sufficient to assure such security? For the historical record, a detailed list of the armaments Iran would have possessed by 1982 are given in Appendix 4. Our military projects were never kept secret. Quite the contrary, they were well known to all. President Carter had reiterated his support of our endeavors at our meetings in Teheran in December 1977, when he had called our nation an "island of stability" in a very troubled part of the world. Iran truly was the only nation capable of maintaining peace and stability in the Mideast. My departure has changed all that. The Soviet invasion of Afghanistan and the terrorist attack in Mecca demonstrate this all too well.

Our assemblage of a formidable military force in the Mideast has resulted in charges of megalomania and of careless spending of Iran's money on arms while my people are deprived of basic needs.

The question of the adequacy of our military forces is subjective. To my knowledge, no military leader of world stature has criticized my arms policy as excessive. As for robbing the Iranian people of their living essentials in order to pay for armaments, nothing could be further from the truth. After paying for these armaments, Iran had a reserve of $12 billion in foreign currency.

11

The Unholy Alliance of Red and Black

THE BLACK AND RED alliance that would prove so destructive goes back far in time and is deeply rooted in Iran's consciousness. The black—the clergy—had opposed my father, and supported my rule only sporadically. Religious fanatics who did not understand the true nature of Islam had allied with the Tudeh back in the 1940s. Our investigation of my would-be assassin, Fakhr Arai in 1949, attested to this confederation. Mossadegh's government demonstrated how such a red-black alliance could thrive without a clear understanding by the noncommunist members of its consequences. In the early fifties, the Tudeh Party was merely biding its time, waiting for Mossadegh to oust me so that it in turn could safely eliminate him. We know this beyond question from documents found in Tudeh's offices after Mossadegh's sudden fall. The situation is no different today. The communists are waiting for Khomeini to lead my country into chaos, poverty, and despair before taking over.

The media, the major oil companies, and the British and American governments were the other ingredients in this strange amalgam. My success in negotiating a 75/25 oil royalty agreement with Enricco Mattei of E.N.I. in 1957 enraged the international oil cartel. Politically, my action showed a greater degree of independence than the Americans and British were willing to tolerate. The British, of course, had always considered Iran as a fiefdom and tried to dominate our national life. The Mossadegh misadventure had brought the Americans onto the scene and given Washington an incentive to intervene.

The results of their combined displeasure became obvious in the late fifties. The first student demonstrations against my regime broke out then, interestingly enough, in the United States. In 1962, while at a ceremony in San Francisco, I saw a plane overhead with a streamer proclaiming "need a fix, see the Shah." Clearly, this was part of an organized effort to discredit me and my government. I cannot help but believe that the oil companies and an organization like the CIA were somehow involved in fomenting and financing this campaign against me. This effort acquired a professional polish over the years that students could not have achieved on their own. It is hard to believe that the KGB was quite that effective in the United States in those days.

For the next twenty years students and media echoed the same anti-Iran themes intermittently, whenever the West felt my wings needed clipping. The late fifties and early sixties were one such period. The years after the oil embargo and the hike in world oil prices were another.

The early sixties were a particularly turbulent time for us. They coincided with the advent of the Kennedy administration and increased U.S. intrigue against our country. Repeatedly, I tried to warn Kennedy of the oil crunch I saw ahead. But the President scoffed at my concerns. At one of our meetings he expressed confidence that even if all Mideast oil were shut off, the U.S. had large enough reserves to meet world needs for two years. It was difficult to argue against such deluded selfconfidence.

In Iran this period was marked by student and teacher demonstrations, by the temporary closing of Teheran University, and by renewed National Front agitation. The U.S. pressed me to name Ali Amini, Mossadegh's Minister of Economics and by then an opposition leader, as prime minister. Sharif Emami, my Prime Minister at the time, warned me against U.S. intrigues but I did not believe him. In May 1961 I gave in and appointed Amini to head the government. Fifteen months later—a time marked by economic and political mismanagement—Amini resigned. Even the Americans had lost faith in his abilities. In better control of the situation, I was finally able to act and to inaugurate the White Revolution, thus winning a decade's respite from my foreign "friends" and domestic enemies.

Well, let us say I won a partial respite. Terrorism has been a feature of Iranian political life for a long time. No matter how hard I tried, and God knows I tried, my country was never quite rid of it. I have already discussed the 1949 attempt on my life and the 1951 murder of my Prime Minister, General Razmara. In late 1955 assassins shot and wounded my then Prime Minister, Hussein Ala. As I previously discussed, I was the victim of a second assassination attempt on April 10, 1965. A young soldier shot his way into the palace. A subsequent investigation showed that he had been part of an extreme left-wing plot masterminded by university people.

On January 21, 1965, Moslem fanatics shot and killed another of my Prime Ministers, Hasan Ali Mansur. Later, several of my generals were killed, and in the early seventies terrorists murdered three American colonels in the streets in Teheran. This mayhem was not only directed at the prominent or public figures. I remember other victims, a taxi driver and a car washer, for example, shot and killed trying to disarm terrorists.

The media, of course, never let an opportunity go to play up acts of violence and to make them reflect badly on my rule. Sometimes they would go to ludicrous lengths. In late 1959 President Eisenhower visited me in Teheran. As is the custom for visiting heads of state both in monarchies and democracies, I had stationed an honor guard along the route from the airport to the palace. The newspapers reported that the Shah feared so much for his life that he put all his soldiers into the streets to protect him. On another occasion in the sixties when we made our annual move to our summer palace on the Caspian Sea, the Western press reported that the Shah has fled Teheran and taken refuge in the North.

Nothing I did could stop these preposterous stories, not the interviews I gave to every foreign journalist who spent any time in my country, not the frequent press conferences open to all media, not my regular appearances on American television, both on trips to the U.S. and from Teheran. Perhaps I was too confident in what I said and how I said it, so at times I may have appeared arrogant. But all I ever wanted was that foreign journalists understand Iran—its history, its problems, its future. Unfortunately, most media people came with preconceived ideas about what Iran was and should be. Too often they based their thinking on Western values. Nevertheless, I always encouraged debates, which permit you to express yourself, and always enjoyed provocative questioning. Unfortunately, the media continually viewed my country through Western eyes. They never looked at Iran as a Middle Eastern nation bordering on the Soviet Union and with a vastly different cultural and religious value system. Thus, they unfairly categorized my regime as repressive. Small wonder that Iranian students abroad, exposed to a steady diet of vilification of their homeland, would also demand that Iran become what it was not, and could not become in so short a time.

The media campaign grew more virulent after the oil embargo and the price hike. The statements of certain American government leaders did not help. Thus, Secretary of the Treasury William Simon called me a "nut" and the media picked up this controversy with glee. Simon's insults led the media to label me as the man responsible for expensive oil. But nobody bothered to explain my reasons for raising oil prices as I detailed earlier.

As a result of this calumny I can well understand the anger of Western drivers as the cost of gasoline rose and shortages appeared. They were simply told it was all the Shah's fault, while few bothered to tell them how much their government's tax revenue rose as a result.

Media attacks, terrorism, student agitation, the beginnings of Western pressure to liberalize my regime, all began to converge on my government in the mid-seventies. Curiously, the clergy were largely silent in those years. Some Moslem extremists dabbled in the left-wing ideologies responsible for part of the terrorist violence, but they were not in the clerical mainstream. When I became Shah, I swore an oath to uphold the constitution and to defend the faith, the Shiite religion of the Twelve Imams. In turn, the clergy recognized me as sovereign and as Defender of the Faith. I am a religious man, a believer; I follow the precepts of the sacred Book of Islam, precepts of balance, justice, and moderation. Nevertheless, there were elements of the clergy during my reign who opposed my reforms and my efforts to modernize Iranian society. We have already seen the violent form that opposition took on occasion, for example during the agrarian reforms of the early sixties. But as late as spring 1978, during my annual pilgrimage to Meshed, I was not only given a warm welcome from the local population, but hundreds of clerics there showed me respect, loyalty, and affection. And this was at a time when some of the mullahs had already joined the subversive moment.

The first signs of organized opposition to my rule came toward the end of 1976 from liberals, left-wingers, and people of wealth and power inside my country. Meanwhile, I had already allowed the International Red Cross, the International Association of Jurists, and Amnesty International to review our criminal justice system. I readily asked for and accepted their comments, criticism, and suggestions. We paid a good deal of attention to some of their recommendations. Needless to say the media reported the alleged abuses in great detail but paid little heed to the changes we made as a result of these missions.

Early in 1977 the terrorism that had shaken our society for so long abruptly stopped. I knew this was no fortuitous accident. Such actions are calculated and carefully thought out and I was convinced that this ominous silence was no exception. If these hardened terrorists who routinely had sprayed the streets with machinegun fire and thus randomly killed innocent men, women, and children had ceased these activities, something else must have started. True, I had "eyes and ears" among the population, but they brought me little in the way of conclusive information so that I was unable to discern the deeper meaning of this cessation of terrorism. From this developed a need for more expeditious changes. Thus, over the next two years the urgency for completion of my reasonable and viable reforms was vastly increased. In this way, I hoped to diffuse my opponents' unreasonable and unrealistic demands for radical changes that my government's infrastructure would not be capable of withstanding.

Their demands for "authentic parliamentary democracy" were in reality nothing more than demagoguery that would result in a caricature of democracy such as has been seen so often in discredited multi-party systems. I wanted a true democracy designed to foster my country's real interests. But my opponents were not interested in that approach. As a result, the more I liberalized, the worse the situation inside Iran became. Every initiative I took was seen as proof of my own weakness and that of my government.

By the summer of 1977 I had a sense of the new troubles ahead. Perhaps my own instincts were more accurate than the information my people gathered in the towns and the countryside. I felt that some political change was needed. Amir Abbas Hoveyda had been Prime Minister since 1965, the longest tenure of any of my heads of government. Hoveyda was a talented and dedicated man. But he too felt that he had been in office too long. In fact, he told me with some relief when I asked him for his resignation that no Prime Minister should serve longer than five years. Since I valued his counsel, I named Hoveyda my Minister of Court and thus was assured of his continued advice on a close, personal basis.

In August 1977, I appointed Namshid Amouzegar Prime Minister. At the time foreign policy issues occupied most of my attention and I thought Amouzegar well suited to handle them. He had represented Iran at OPEC for a number of years and acquitted himself with distinction during the tough, arduous sessions of that body. Moreover, he had completed his engineering studies in the United States and still had good friends in that country. In Iran he enjoyed a reputation for integrity. As the Resurgence Party's general secretary, he had a political base of his own. Finally, his appointment could serve as a springboard for a new liberalization drive that would promote democracy within Iran. I wanted to avoid a general collapse which I knew would ensue if liberal and leftist demands were realized.

That autumn in a *Newsweek* interview I had the opportunity to reiterate for the public's attention an apparently forgotten agreement between the U.S. and Iran, as well as to raise in the West's consciousness of the Soviet Union's dogged determination to dominate the world. In that interview with Arnaud de Borchgrave I discussed the bilateral agreement signed on March 5, 1959, by the U.S. and Iran. I noted that by this agreement the U.S. considered Iran's independence vital to its own national interest and therefore would furnish military assistance to Iran. The U.S. also committed itself to come to Iran's assistance if we were attacked, although this latter commitment was couched in vague diplomatic terms—that is, it merely stated appropriate action would be taken when mutually agreed upon. I also expressed my concerns about the West's determination to fight Soviet aggression. I noted that it is becoming increasingly difficult to discern just at what point the U.S. would be willing to stand up and fight. This interview also afforded me the opportunity to discuss the North-South problem and the growing debt of underdeveloped nations. I said then and still strongly believe that though the West may not be in a position to wipe out these debts, a new deal must be struck with the underdeveloped countries. Ten percent of the world's population cannot for long control 90 percent of its riches without world upheaval. Redistribution is not the answer; creation of "new" sources of wealth is the basic need of the developing nations today. Cooperation by all developed nations—East and West alike—is vital to this effort.

Our foreign difficulties were highlighted during our visit to the U.S. later that fall. As usual on these official visits, the Empress and I spent a night in Williamsburg, Virginia, to tour the historic restorations. Several hundred Iranian students had gathered near my hotel to express their loyalty. I stopped to chat briefly with the group when I noted a smaller knot of people, most of them masked, standing around a red flag complete with hammer and sickle. They hurled insults at us. Why the masks? I would learn in the next day's newspapers that these demonstrators feared the SAVAK. A more likely explanation than that ridiculous charge, it seemed to me, was that the masks hid non-Iranian demonstrators—professional troublemakers hired on the spot. In any event, the anti-Shah protesters could not have numbered more than fifty while my supporters were close to five hundred.

Imagine my amazement the next day when I saw the press had reversed the numbers and wrote that the fifty Shah supporters were lost in a hostile crowd. A similar reversal appeared in print during our visit to Washington. This time the demonstrations were larger and more violent. A crowd of several thousand Iranians living in the U.S. had gathered to greet us on the Ellipse south of the White House. They sat on hastily erected bleachers and had hoisted a huge white banner that said: "Welcome Shah." A much smaller group of demonstrators, several hundred at the most, had gathered in Lafayette Park on the other side of the Executive Mansion. Again, they wore masks and carried placards explaining that "Masks Protect Us From SAVAK."

After we had arrived for the welcoming ceremonies on the south lawn of the White House, the "student" demonstrators charged the peaceful assembly of my supporters. They swung placard handles and planks armed with nails. The police were not prepared for the violence and gave way, using tear gas in an effort to restore order. More than 130 persons were injured before the riot was over. Again the media switched the figures. *Time,* for example, wrote that a thousand "opponents of the Shah" had gathered in Lafayette Park to face "several hundred of the Shah's supporters," even though the opposite numbers were correct. Nor did the U.S. press chastise the aggressors. One newspaper wrote meaningfully, "Who, then, paid for the Shah's supporters to come to America?" Another charged that my government had paid their expenses and additionally gave each supporter a $100 bill. There was, of course, not a word of truth to the allegations. On the other hand, no one bothered to investigate the troublemakers' sources of support.

I know that very few of them were Iranians. Most of them were young Americans—blonde, blacks, Puerto Ricans, together with some Arabs. Moreover, there was foreign money involved in paying their bills. I had reports at the time of a dummy foundation set up in New York with money sent from Europe and other places to pay for anti-Shah demonstrators to come to Washington. Buses had been organized to bring people from New York and other cities. And I know that many other demonstrators were flown in from as far away as Los Angeles. These were facts no one bothered to report. The press was too busy detailing my alleged human rights violations or reporting that "the Shah's political jails hold 25,000 to 100,000 political prisoners."

In all fairness, however, *Time* did report that I had embarked on a program of liberalization and that Prime Minister Amouzegar had moved to end press censorship, had loosened controls, and had freed several hundred political prisoners. "In a few months," *Time* wrote in November 1977, "the police-state atmosphere has altered drastically to a mood of vastly greater individual freedom and relaxation." This report came fifteen months before my ouster!

My talks with President Carter had gone well. Iran's relationship with the U.S. had been so deep and so friendly during the last three Administrations—I had counted Lyndon Johnson, Richard Nixon and Gerald Ford among my friends—that it seemed only natural that our friendship would continue. After all, good relations were in the best interests of both nations. Carter appeared to be a smart man.

My favorable impression of the new American President deepened when he visited Teheran to spend New Year's Eve with us at Niavaran Palace. I have never heard a foreign statesman speak of me in quite such flattering terms as he used that evening. "Iran, because of the great leadership of the Shah, is an island of stability in one of the more troubled areas of the world," Carter said in his prepared remarks at dinner. He went on to say:

> "Our talks have been priceless, our friendship is irreplaceable, and my own gratitude is to the Shah, who in his wisdom and with his experience has been so helpful to me, a new leader."

A week later, on January 7, 1978, the first riots erupted in which the clergy were the major source of the agitation. Demonstrators surged through the streets of the holy city of Qom where thousands of pilgrims annually visit the tomb of Massoumeh, the sister of Imam Reza. There is little doubt in my mind that communist elements had infiltrated the 4,000 religious students and their supporters who took part in the protest. I am equally certain that rebellious and dissatisfied mullahs were at the center of the unrest. Six people were killed during the disturbance, a number duly exaggerated in media accounts of the incident to dozens of dead and hundreds of injured. The renewal of violence after a year's calm troubled me. I realized that political agitation in Iran was entering a new phase, that the conspirators, whatever their origins, had changed their tactics and we were now faced with organized violence.

As a counter to this demonstration, a crowd of 30,000 paraded through Qom some days later to express their support for my government and my rule, but it was already too late. That first demonstration in Qom gave the mullahs their martyrs and soon they were able to spread a refined and sophisticated "bereavement" technique to other cities. According to Moslem tradition, parents and friends of the deceased gather at the tomb forty days after the death. SAVAK "victims" were produced enmasse as a pretext for holding such graveside assemblies. My opponents seized corpses from grieving families and paraded them through city streets, shouting: "Here is another victim of the regime, another of SAVAK's crimes." Many of those carried on the shoulders of demonstrators had died from natural causes. Some were Jews whose religious laws require burial within 24 hours of death and whose beliefs were carelessly trampled by malcontents intent on fraud and violence. They had only one aim—to trigger daily demonstrations which were ever more frequent once the forty-day mourning cycle had been established. Of course, these protests were always accompanied by more violence and often by more deaths, creating a self-perpetuating cycle of destruction.

It is hard to imagine any more vile behavior by supposed religious people than those upheavals of 1978. These insurgents often pretended to be wounded and had themselves daubed with mercurochrome to appear battered and bloody—especially when unscrupulous news photographers were on the scene.

The next wave of violence hit the city of Tabriz in the riots of February 18, and soon reached the holy cities of Qom and Meshed. These were contained, but it took considerable force to do so, perhaps too much force. On March 5 my government disciplined some police and SAVAK officials for the way they had handled the riots. This shows, incidentally, that SAVAK was never allowed to operate unchecked in Iran. As the riots spread, underlying social issues began to emerge. The unholy alliance of red and black was beginning to solidify. Looking back, the uprisings in Tabriz marked the beginning of efforts to reduce my authority, to turn me into a weak and ineffectual "constitutional" monarch, and finally to oust me.

True, under my rule Iran had progressed at a rapid pace. The growth of Teheran in a few years from a city of one million to a metropolis of 4.5 million could not be accomplished without some social and economic dislocation. There were plenty of jobs. When I left my country, a million foreign workers were employed at all levels of the economy. (Under Khomeini's government, all the foreign workers have left and more than four million Iranians are unemployed.) Housing construction could not keep up with demand. Thus, real estate prices rose to dizzying heights as they have in other major cities gripped by housing shortages, and many fortunes were made. Luxury apartments dotted the cityscape. My push for construction of low-income housing lagged because production of brick and cement could not keep pace with our needs. This problem was compounded by bottlenecks at our ports; imported cement spoiled at dockside.

But the situation had not yet slipped out of my control. Popular support for the crown ran strong and deep. In spring of 1978 I traveled to the holy city of Meshed. The warmth of my welcome was overwhelming. I drove in an open car at not more than five miles an hour while crowds pressed close to me. My security was minimal. There could have been a sniper behind any window. My reception in Meshed was not an isolated incident. When Prime Minister Amouzegar visited the provinces several weeks later, his reception was equally tumultuous. In Tabriz, so hard hit by the February riots, 300,000 turned out to cheer the head of the government.

Nelson Rockefeller visited me that spring. Times were ominous, not only in Iran. Across the border in Afghanistan, the communists had quietly taken control of a neutralist government, with few in the West aware or concerned. For ten years I had been warning the West about Afghanistan, her strategic importance, and her unstable politics; but my warnings were ignored. It is worth noting here that had I remained in power, the Russians would not have dared invade Afghanistan. By January 1980, Iran would have had a standing army of 700,000 men equipped with the most modern weaponry available and supported by F-15 and F-16 fighter-bombers. It is very doubtful that the Red Army would have challenged this force.

This was one of the issues Rockefeller and I discussed. We were old friends. He was no longer in office and could talk freely. "Is it conceivable," I asked him pointblank, "that the Americans and the Russians have divided the world between them?" "Of course not," he replied. And added, "At least as far as I know . . ."

In mid-March disturbances had swept through several cities including Teheran. However, the next two months proved quiet. I began to hope that the worst was over. In mid-May the deceptive calm shattered. Students went on strike. The bazaars closed. The links among students, merchants, and clergy tightened. Much has been made of *bazaaris* opposition to my rule and their relationship with the mullahs.

Some Western accounts have alleged that the CIA had been paying between $400–450 million annually to Iran's clergy and that in 1977 Carter ordered this assistance ceased. I have no knowledge of any CIA support of our mullahs. For some time my government had been providing our clergy with substantial support. In 1977 due to the exigencies of our economy, Prime Minister Amouzegar was forced to eliminate these payments. Western analysts have theorized that these actions precipitated an organized rebellion of the clergy. Other stories allege that the bazaaris revolted against my government because we had moved to impose price controls, a vital effort to curb inflation, and because we had pushed to develop Western-style supermarkets and shopping malls at the expense of the bazaars.

In retrospect, I regret Amouzegar's actions in these areas. But I cannot subscribe to these Western postulates that they were prime factors in the overthrow of my government. Too many other factors were involved.

The fight against inflation, for example, dated back to the mid-seventies. As we have seen, the crackdown although justified, entailed hardship. In August 1975, some 8,000 price gougers were tried in our courts. We had hired students to check on merchant compliance with price guidelines. We had counted on their incorruptibility, but many of them may have been too zealous. Others were probably saboteurs who saw in these jobs an opportunity to sow dissension and foment trouble. Our price controls were imposed across the economy; the bazaars were not singled out.

Bazaars are a major social and commercial institution throughout the Mideast. But it remains my conviction that their time is past. The bazaar consists of a cluster of small shops. There is usually little sunshine or ventilation so that they are basically unhealthy environs. The bazaaris are a fanatic lot, highly resistant to change because their locations afford a lucrative monopoly. I could not stop building supermarkets. I wanted a modern country. Moving against the bazaars was typical of the political and social risks I had to take in my drive for modernization.

As I continued to liberalize the opposition grew increasingly vocal and organized. Unfortunately, the press focused not on their actions but on SAVAK.

The very worst crimes have been attributed to SAVAK. It has been alleged that millions of Iranians were employed by it. In fact, at the end of 1978, SAVAK employed less than 4,000 people.

The name SAVAK comes from the initials in Persian of the Organization for State Security and Information. Similar organizations exist worldwide since every country is obliged to protect its populace from subversion. Accordingly they are called KGB, CIA or FBI, Intelligence Service, M15, or SDECE.

Is it necessary to add that Iran has no more reason to tolerate terrorism than the Italians have to tolerate the activities of the Red Brigades or the Germans the demands of the Baader Meinhof gang? And when in Germany, six prisoners commit suicide all on the same day, by aiming bullets into the backs of their necks to be sure of success, barely any surprise is shown at their having firearms in their cells. This series of altogether peculiar coincidences is regarded as perfectly normal. World public opinion accepts the story without a frown.

SAVAK was instituted in Iran to combat communist subversion after the disastrous Mossadegh episode. It is not for me to judge the attitude adopted by Western countries towards their communists. However, a common frontier with the Soviet Union tends to sharpen one's perceptions of their activities.

Although I managed to have neighborly relations with Russia, as well as advantageous economic cooperation, we did pass through difficult times immediately after the war. Remember that the Soviet troops who occupied our country in World War II only left it in April 1946 and that the Tudeh party really thought its hour had come during the last months of Mossadegh's rule. Thus, we were obliged to outlaw this party which threatened not only the regime, but the country's territorial integrity.

SAVAK was created, then, to put an end to these subversive activities. The organization was first headed by General Bakhtiar in 1953, and he called in the CIA to advise him. Subsequently many SAVAK officials went to the U.S. for training by the CIA. They also went to Great Britain and other Western countries to observe their operations.

General Bakhtiar kept this position until 1962, when his ambitions and inquisitorial methods interfered with his effectiveness in office. He was exiled and several years later he was assassinated in Iraq.

There were in Iran, as elsewhere, traitors, spies, agitators, and professional saboteurs, about whom our government and military leaders required intelligence. This was SAVAK's responsibility. As an information and counterespionage organization it originally served civil magistrates. But as a result of recommendations made by international human rights groups, this function was left to the ordinary police force.

The officers of SAVAK were trusted soldiers who recruited agents from the army, the police, and university graduates. But the majority of its staff were civilians. Although this force at one time alone handled the questioning procedure in our judicial process, by late 1978 on the advice of international lawyers, this was modified so that defense lawyers participated in the proceedings.

SAVAK's activities were exaggerated by insurrectionists to further incite the nation. According to "informants" the number of "political prisoners" and people being "tortured" in our prisons fluctuated between 25,000 and 100,000. Now in *Chronicles of the Repression*, a clandestine paper printed in Iran and used by the opposition against SAVAK, it was specified that between 1968 and 1977, that is over nine years, the number of people *arrested* for political reasons was exactly 3,164.

Our Prime Minister was directly responsible for the day-to-day operations of SAVAK. As head of state, I could only intervene at the request of the Minister of Justice to exercise the Right of Pardon over condemned men. However, when I learned that torture and abuse existed, as a matter of policy I ordered it stopped.

I was deeply moved when I heard that before being tortured and assassinated, Mr. Hoveyda, the former Prime Minister, and the former heads of SAVAK, Generals Pakravan, Nassiri, and Moghadam had insisted that they had never received any order whatsoever from me with regard to a suspect, an accused man, or a condemned one.

I had the power to commute sentences, which I always used as widely as possible. I signed all applications for pardon or remission of sentences which the magistrates presented to me. As for those who made attempts on my life, I always pardoned them, even against the advice of the Public Prosecutor.

I cannot defend SAVAK's every action and will not attempt to do so here. There were people arrested and abused. Unfortunately, this is not a perfect world. Worldwide police brutality exists. Inherent in police work is the potential for abuse and cruelty. My country, too, fell victim to such excesses. However, whenever I learned of abuse, I put an end to it. When the International Red Cross wished to investigate, the prisons were opened to their representatives. Their recommendations were followed.

I must draw a distinction here between terrorists and political prisoners. It was inevitable that some terrorists died in confrontation with SAVAK and local police. No one forced them to start fires, to pillage, and to murder. They were the victims of their own choice.

With regard to those who were arrested for political reasons—I cannot include arsonists and saboteurs in this category—I affirm that they were properly treated and that they were never molested in any way. No one can tell me the name of a single politician who has been "liquidated" by SAVAK.

In June 1978 I replaced the long-time head of SAVAK, General Nassiri, with General Moghadam, who was more a philosopher than a soldier and from whose benign attitude I expected beneficial results. Again, I would be sadly disappointed. Riots shook the holy city of Meshed on July 22. Clerical unrest was growing and from Iraq Khomeini increased his attacks. Cassettes of his speeches and harangues were smuggled into our country and used by his supporters to incite the masses.

Hoping to stem the rising violence, I announced on August 5, 1978, our Constitution Day, that free elections would take place at the end of the current parliamentary session, in the spring of 1979. The elections would culminate my steady drive to create a true democracy in Iran. Thus, the polls would be open to anyone, including those opposed to the present government. My announcement of open elections was followed by riots in Isfahan, Shiraz, and Teheran, proof positive that the opposition was not interested in a more democratic government. Their sole aim and interest was the overthrow of my regime. I am convinced that if these free elections had taken place, the country would have clearly pronounced itself in favor of the democratic government for which we had laid the foundations. It is because we were reaching this goal that an alliance of destructive forces took place against us. It is thus that one sees the representatives of certain *bazaaris* and a pseudotheocratic feudalism joining hands with parties and sects of the extreme left.

The situation in Isfahan grew so violent that the government had to impose martial law there. My opponents could not afford to relax their agitation lest common sense prevail and persuade their naive followers of the folly of their actions. No matter how often I reaffirmed my commitment to liberalization, the answer was always the same: more riots.

On August 19, fire swept a cinema in Abadan killing 477 people. Many were burned alive, others asphyxiated. The fires were set deliberately in an act of brutal mass murder. Immediately my government was blamed for this atrocious act. Supposedly, the police had locked the doors of the cinema so that no one could escape. We were also charged with having started the fire. Khomeini needed yet another provocation to whet the appetites of his fanatic following.

The real culprit fled to Iraq, where he was arrested. He confessed, but frightened or pusillanimous magistrates covered up the affair. The arrested man alone could say on whose behalf he committed this outrage.

Popular reaction, fulfilled the instigators' every dream. Rioting swept the country and raged for several days. At the height of this upheaval, General Moghadam came to see me. He had just met with one of the major religious leaders. His message for me: Do something spectacular! He had repeated that word, "spectacular" several times.

Under the circumstances, I wondered what dramatic action I could take to save the country from chaos and destruction. Perhaps a new government might provide the answer, a government to which I would relinquish my own powers. I discussed this possibility with Prime Minister Amouzegar and he promptly offered me his resignation. I accepted—a great mistake on my part. I never should have allowed this wise and unbiased counselor to withdraw. On August 27, I named Sharif Emami, who had been Prime Minister twenty years before, to head a new government.

He tried to disassociate his government from the past in an effort to win a new start for himself and his cabinet. He denounced the Resurgence Party, a move which failed to appease the opposition, but succeeded in cutting off that party's support for his government. Emami also tried to curry favor with Shiite clergy, by reintroducing the old Hegira calendar and ordering all casinos and gambling clubs closed. This too proved ineffectual.

Street rioting continued. By September 8, it had reached such proportions that Emami was forced to impose martial law in Teheran. Under our Constitution, such an action must be approved by the Majlis within a week of its imposition. Accordingly, on September 10, Emami requested and received the required approval—for eleven other cities as well as Teheran. That very day he and his cabinet also were given a vote of confidence by the Majlis. That September 8 would become known as "Black Friday." The violence of that Friday's demonstrations reached such a pitch of murder, pillage, and arson that the security forces had no choice but to fire. The death toll of 86 was reported by the Teheran Martial Law Office on September 10, the very day the Majlis confirmed the new government. Emami stated publicly that he took full responsibility for the consequences of martial law.

For all the bloodshed and despite all the vilification heaped on our police and soldiers, I must pay tribute to the *sang-froid* they showed. Uncontrolled mobs who had savagely murdered their comrades in arms failed to provoke them into equally bloody revenge. Moreover, martial law was not strictly enforced. Its imposition was little more than a warning. Riots continued and insurgents paid little heed to the troops who in fact fired only on arsonists, pillagers, or armed saboteurs.

The Camp David meetings on the Middle East were underway as unrest mounted in Iran. I have been told that some Americans, Israelis, and Egyptians taking part in those meetings expressed considerable concern about the events in my country. Some reports suggested that Israeli spokesmen told the Americans that Iran was more important than their own negotiations. If so, I had no knowledge of it, nor did these warnings have much effect on American action. President Sadat's concern had equally little effect. Sadat called me late on the night of September 9 and we talked for a few minutes. As always, Sadat offered his encouragement and his help. I have no way of knowing what he said to President Carter later that night. But I do know that reports widely circulated in the West about a Carter telephone call to me later that night are false. President Carter has never called me—except once at Lackland Air Force Base in December 1979.

In early September, the American ambassador, William Sullivan, returned from holiday to his post in Teheran. In any number of interviews Mr. Sullivan has given since my exile—and his own retirement from the U.S. Foreign Service—he has said that he knew in September 1978 that I could not survive. He has told this to the *International Herald Tribune* and anyone else who would listen. But he never told me. For the next four months the only word I ever received from Mr. Sullivan was reiteration of Washington's complete support for my rule. To be more specific, the U.S. backed me 100 percent and hoped I would establish law and order, as well as continue my program of political liberalization.

For the balance of the year I received numerous messages from various people in and out of the Carter Administration pledging U.S. support. Whenever I met Sullivan and asked him to confirm these official statements, he promised he would. But a day or two later he would return, gravely shake his head and say that he had received "no instructions" and therefore could not comment. Sullivan appeared to me always polite, always grave, always concerned. He came to see me several times a week. He seemed to take seriously everything I said to him. But his answer was always the same: I have received no instructions. Is it any wonder that I felt increasingly isolated and cut off from my Western friends? What were they really thinking, what did they want—for Iran and of me? I was never told. I never knew. Sullivan, and the British ambassador, Anthony Parsons, who so often accompanied him, met in a stiff diplomatic ballet that ended without resolution of any kind. Meanwhile, I was forced to deal with what is usually described as a prerevolutionary situation. In truth, it was the end of modern civilization in Iran.

The mosques had become hotbeds of dissent. Street riots were orchestrated by the mullahs. For the first time the slogans of Islamic Marxism were trumpeted before large audiences. The Mujahidin-e Khalq (Fighters for the People)—saboteurs trained in Lebanon and Libya—took this surprising theory to our naive masses who listened with interest for the first time; the agitators now had the backing of the mullahs and thus the blessing of organized religion for their preposterous statements.

How can communists, plutocratic *bazaaris*, and Islamic clergy join hands in the same revolution? One cannot imagine such divergent philosophies coalescing. The responsibility for this union rests upon the shoulders of those prelates who naively put their hands in those of militant atheists. At present, they feel obliged to make a higher revolutionary bid, to show themselves as being more demagogic, more pitiless, and more destructive than their "fellow travelers" whose prisoners and hostages they will ultimately become. They can only denounce in vain this fatal alliance, for they are doomed to advance on its cursed path.

These prelates have compromised themselves. Tomorrow they will find themselves isolated. Then as is the rule in the Marxist universe, they have to surrender and no one will defend them. They will leave their mark upon history only through the crimes which they were forced to commit and for which they took frightful responsibility "in the name of God." The tragedy is that religion will be obliterated by militant atheism, in the name of the Sovereign People and the Communist Gospels.

The Western press continues to play the communist game—they claim that bloodshed and death that marred our cities had nothing to do with terrorists but was the work of SAVAK agents and the police. If SAVAK had only been as effective as my enemies claimed, they would not have been out in the streets shouting vilifications. By November 1978 our total prison population was only 300—this in a nation of 35 million! But the Western press continued to accept blindly Khomeini's figures of 100,000.

By October it became increasingly clear that careful plans had been made for the collapse of Iran. In the larger towns where martial law was still in force, terrorist groups, armed with automatic rifles and explosives, battled troops and police. They moved with the stealth of classic urban guerrillas. Soon they attacked government offices and foreign embassies. Confrontation grew more ominous and more dangerous.

On October 5 Iraq expelled Khomeini and he flew to France where he took up refuge in the village of Neauphle-le-Château near Paris. Should I have stopped the move and persuaded the Iraqi government to keep him? The question is a difficult one to answer. It is true the French government asked me at the time whether I had any objections to Khomeini's change of venue. I did not, believing that he could do as much damage from Hamburg or Zurich as he could from Paris and that I lacked the power to line up the world in a solid phalanx against a frail and crazy old man. I could hear the thunder in the Western media should I attempt any action so harsh and autocratic.

Under these most difficult and trying conditions, I continued to push reforms and liberalization to prepare the country for free elections. I moved against corruption on a broad basis. Businessmen and officials who had enriched themselves illegally were arrested and I fully intended to bring them to trial. In a little-noticed action that summer I had issued a code of conduct for my own family as insurance against slander and calumny. Censorship was lifted: Newspapers were free once again to print what they liked; Iranian television broadcast parliamentary debates during which opposition deputies made fiery antigovernment speeches. Parliament, I thought, was a much more appropriate forum in which to voice dissent than the streets of our cities.

But the war on the streets continued. After Khomeini left for Paris, so-called students again used their "bereavement" tactics to confront the authorities. Rioting broke out in many of the provinces; demonstrators went on a rampage. Banks, ministries, and businesses were set afire, windows of schools and offices were broken, banks, shops and restaurants were looted. Police and security guards were forced to fire on the crowds in order to end this senseless vandalism and rioting and to restore peace. At the end of the first week in October, strikers succeeded in shutting down government ministries and closing airports and schools. On the 16th a crowd of 100,000 marched through Teheran to protest the victims of "Black Friday," again exaggerating the number of dead and wounded. For the first time I began to detect a defeatist tone in the conversations of the British and American ambassadors. I suggested holding a pro-Shah rally. My people were sure that such a rally would be a huge show of force and strength for the Crown. The envoys shrugged and said what is the point in that? The next day the opposition will have double that number opposing you. It is a race you cannot win. I believed them then, I now know I was wrong. I could have won such a contest.

Sharif Emami's government began to weaken. The concessions it had offered had been too few and mostly ill-chosen. The Americans began to push the idea of a coalition government. Why not bring in members of the opposition, specifically the leaders of the old National Front of Mossadegh's day? Reaching out across political barriers, they said, could re-establish badly frayed national unity. I tried. I contacted Karim Sanjabi and several other opposition leaders. But their demands were unacceptable. Shortly thereafter Sanjabi and Mehdi Bazargan, a rich lawyer and human rights "activist" who would head Khomeini's first government, visited the aged mullah in his French retreat. Other efforts to broaden the government's political base failed, although on the day before my 59th birthday, October 26, I freed another 1,500 political prisoners and later eliminated those undesirables from SAVAK who had been brought to my attention.

Strikes spread—at the end of October oil workers began to walk out and paralyze our $20 billion oil industry. Oil production began a dizzying fall from more than 6 million barrels a day to barely 1.5 million. Air Iran went on strike again. More riots swept the capital on November 5. Loudspeakers were set up on university campuses and in secondary schools to broadcast messages of hate and rage. University and high school students responded by joining "Islamic Revolution" activists in the streets. Army and police were ordered to contain the demonstrations but to shoot only if absolutely necessary. Banks, cinemas, public buildings, and hotels in the capital's western and central districts were sacked and burned. Soldiers guarding the British embassy could not stop an attacking mob and had to watch the building burn, destroying a part of the complex. The Information Ministry was besieged and sacked.

The messages I received from the United States while all this was going on continued to be confusing and contradictory. Secretary of State Vance issued a statement endorsing my efforts to restore calm and encouraging the liberalization program. Such Herculean fantasies left me stunned. President Carter's National Security Advisor, Zbigniew Brzezinski, at least had his priorities straight. He called me in early November to urge that I establish law and order first, and only then continue our democratization program.

That call, too, has become famous, although at least it actually happened. What followed, however, was truly bizarre. I thanked Brzezinski for his expressions of support. The next day I sought confirmation of the message from Ambassador Sullivan. As usual the American envoy promised to cable Washington, but when I next saw him, he said gravely that he had received no instructions. This rote answer had been given me since early September and I would continue to hear it until the day I left the country.

Since then I have often been asked why I did not seek the confirmation I wanted through other channels, perhaps by picking up the telephone and calling Washington. My answer is simple. In foreign affairs, I have always observed the protocal of international diplomacy. Thus, I never tried to establish direct contact with Carter or anyone else in the Administration because that is done through an ambassador. The fact that no one contacted me during the crisis in any official way explains everything about the American attitude. I did not know it then—perhaps I did not want to know—but it is clear to me now that the Americans wanted me out. Certainly this was what the human-rights champions in the State Department wanted, and Secretary Vance apparently acceded. I say apparently because again I was never told anything: nothing about the split within the Carter Administration over Iran policy; nothing about the hopes some U.S. officials put in the viability of an "Islamic Republic" as a bulwark against communist incursions. Instead, my ambassador in Washington, Zahedi, reported the same thing I heard day after day from Sullivan in Teheran: The U.S. is a hundred percent behind you. I was ill-served by Ardeshir Zahedi's inaccurate reporting. He had been in Washington too long and was closely identified with the Nixon and Ford Administrations. He pretended to have access to the highest authorities but his reports could never be confirmed. His outgoing temperament was unsuited to the straight-laced Carter White House and I should have replaced him. In any event, protocal was not observed and I was not told the truth.

On November 5 Sharif Emami's position had become untenable and I asked for his resignation. There was little choice left but a military government. None of the opposition politicians I had contacted showed any interest in forming a new cabinet. In fact, few civilians did. I therefore turned to my chief of staff, General Gholam Reza Azhari, an honest, loyal man who had always avoided politics. He accepted as duty the weight of this office. He, too, was anxious to prove his goodwill to the opposition, and he immediately arrested twelve highly-placed officials, among them Mr. Hoveyda, whom he put under house arrest. He told me that only a proper trial could fairly deal with the accusations against my former Prime Minister and the other arrested men.

I was not totally convinced of the wisdom of this assessment, but Mr. Hoveyda, who still has my wholehearted esteem, was one of the favorite targets of the opposition. Knowing that in fact it was I whom they hoped to reach through him, I suggested that he go abroad for awhile, and offered him the Belgian Embassy. Too sure of himself, or perhaps too loyal, he refused. I have mentioned elsewhere the abominable way in which he was treated before his execution.

During the first days of the Azhari government, we still had hope. Work began again and the daily production of oil, which had fallen very low, rose again to 5.3 million barrels a day. There were favorable reactions from the people. The general strike dictated from Neuphle-le-Château for Tuesday, November 12, was a failure. In all the big cities (Teheran, Isfahan, Meshed, Shiraz, and Tabriz), large numbers of young men, armed with clubs, confronted the Red and Black urban guerrillas.

But we wanted peace and the reconciliation of all Iranians. We had liberated, on four or five occasions, several hundred political prisoners; in December, General Azhari reaffirmed the government's declaration of October 19, 1978, that a full amnesty would be granted to all Iranians provided they respected the Constitution. Furthermore, we did everything possible to discourage what might have amounted to counter-terrorism by our own partisans. We freed the last political prisoners; our jails then held only those who had been convicted of murder and other serious crimes.

All too soon it was no longer a question of an opposition conspiracy against me; all the forces of destruction were united. Modern, progressive Iran was to be annihilated, and with it, by one means or another, the representative of a dynasty which had so often saved the country from ruin.

Then began the strikes which were to bring the country to her knees. We had power cuts lasting several hours each day; water and oil were cut off. Transport workers struck; then banks and the most important ministries were closed one after another. Combined, these stoppages paralyzed the nation. Idle crowds thronged the streets, growing all the while more bitter. The ringleaders had threatened most workers, either personally or through their families. It is well known that a mere five or six people inside a big power station can halt supplies of electricity; this is also true of the oil-pumping centers. The effectiveness of such small cadres explains the success of the strikes. In two months, strikes at the oil wells and refineries caused incalculable losses.

Our last effort to hold the country together was on the verge of failure. General Azhari did his best, I know. He felt that he had to placate the opposition. He would rise to speak in Parliament and begin with some verses from the Koran; he tailored his speeches to fit the religious mood and soon was talking like a priest. Soon people began calling him Ayatollah Azhari. Eventually, the strain proved too much and he suffered an incapacitating heart attack.

Since leaving my country I have often asked, and indeed wondered myself, whether stronger action on my part could have saved my throne and my country. Certainly my generals urged me often enough to use force in order to re-establish law and order in the streets. I know today that had I then ordered my troops to shoot, the price in blood would have been a hundred times less severe than that which my people have paid since the establishment of the so-called Islamic Republic. But even that fact does not resolve my fundamental dilemma—a sovereign may not save his throne by shedding his countrymen's blood. A dictator can, for he acts in the name of an ideology and believes it must triumph no matter what the cost. But a sovereign is not a dictator. He cannot break the alliance that exists between him and his people. A dictator has nothing to bestow for power resides in him alone. A sovereign is given a crown and must bequeath it to the next generation. This was my intention. Under my rule, Iran had reached a certain cultural, industrial, agricultural, and technological level. I still hoped to raise these levels before abdicating, so my son, Crown Prince Reza, could reign over a nation, strong industrially, militarily, and culturally, with a growing nuclear industry and no longer as dependent on oil.

During those final weeks I spent most of my time on the telephone with local administrators. The instructions I gave were always the same: "Do the impossible to avoid bloodshed."

One day the mayor of Meshed told me with some embarrassment that mobs in his city were attempting to knock down my statue. I let him know that in light of the bloodshed and mayhem facing us, the forces of law and order were not to be wasted in defense of a statue.

Throughout the period of turmoil and violence that marked the last months of my reign, I wanted to believe that my opponents were of good faith. Did they want more liberalization? I had already effected it. Did they denounce corruption? I had not waited for their demands to act vigorously in this area.

A lawful solution without bloodshed remained my aim. If a climate of conciliation could be established, it might be possible, still, to form that elusive coalition government with members of the opposition. And such a government might succeed in claiming the agitators and their mesmerized mobs. Most importantly, such a government could put the country back to work.

Soon after Prime Minister Azhari's cabinet was confirmed, I resumed discussions with opposition leaders. I first contacted Dr. Sadighi, a member of the National Front, whom I considered a patriot. He agreed without conditions to try to form a coalition, but asked for a week of reflection to which I agreed. Then, acceding to the pressures from his party, he demanded that I nominate a Regency Council while remaining in my country. This condition was unacceptable because it implied that I was incompetent to perform my duties as a sovereign. (It should be noted, however, that Dr. Sadighi was the only political leader who begged me not to leave Iran.) Mr. Sanjabi and Mr. Bazargan had, on returning to Teheran from meetings with Khomeini in France, launched a virulent antigovernment campaign. As a result, Azhari had them arrested for anticonstitutional declarations. From his prison, Mr. Sanjabi asked to see me. He chose as his intermediary General Maghadam, the head of SAVAK, who incidentally was the same man who had brought me the message from the religious leader under the Amouzegar government. For his pains, Moghadam was executed soon after the so-called Islamic Republic was founded.

Determined to do all within my power to effect concilitation, I obtained the freedom of both Mr. Sanjabi and Mr. Bazargan after a few days of detention. I received Mr. Sanjabi shortly thereafter. When he arrived he kissed my hand, declared his personal loyalty to me with great fervor, and announced his readiness to form a government, provided I left Iran for a "vacation."

For him there was no question of naming beforehand a Regency Council, which was constitutionally necessary, nor of asking for a vote of confidence from the Majlis before my departure. I had to reject this solution and seek new consultations which proved to be difficult since the situation continued to deteriorate.

Were these politicians not aware that Iran teetered on the brink of an abyss? Did they not understand that it was no longer a question of safeguarding privileges, monopolies, or the supremacy of one political party over another, but of the life or death of our country?

Economic disorder was everywhere and this was no less worrisome than the agitation in the streets and around the universities. Strike followed strike. Oil production which normally was 5.8 million barrels a day had fallen by December 25 to 1.7 million barrels, a disaster for our economy. Deliveries of natural gas to the Soviet Union were seriously hampered. Clearly, such political and economic chaos could not continue for much longer.

It was at this time that I increasingly questioned my allies' actions: Did the U.S. still hold to our bilateral agreement that obligated them to come to our aid in case we were attacked by a communist country? Did they want it annulled? But as I have already indicated the only answer the American ambassador brought back to my question was the implacable "I have no instructions" or "we support you 100 percent." And even though Sullivan came often with Anthony Parsons, the British envoy, and both made much of the fact that at this time—unlike in the Mossadegh period—the U.S. and Great Britain spoke as one, I found in these sentiments little solace, many doubts.

The messages I received from the Americans continued to be confusing and contradictory. What was I to make, for example, of the Administration's sudden decision to call former Under Secretary of State George Ball to the White House as an advisor on Iran. I knew that Ball was no friend and I understood that he was working on a special report concerning Iran. No one ever informed me what areas the report was to cover, let alone its conclusions. I read them months later in exile and found my worst fears confirmed. Ball was among those Americans who wanted to abandon me and ultimately my country.

Indeed, it almost seemed as if the Russians were more concerned about Iran than the Americans.

The Soviet attiutude toward the upheavals in Iran were succinctly stated in an article published in *Pravda* late in November. In effect, it told the U.S. and the West not to interfere in our internal affairs.

Shortly thereafter, the U.S. indirectly acceded to the Soviet position and issued an official announcement which stated that under no circumstances would the United States interfere in Iran. What had become of our bilateral agreement? When the British and American ambassadors again came to assure me of their continued support, I wondered what I was to conclude from these mixed messages. The West still urged me to continue my liberalization program, while maintaining law and order. Unfortunately, liberalization with a gun pointed at one's head has inherent limitations. I had been in favor of greater freedoms and had implemented policies designed to speed up the democratization process. But the heedless, pell mell rush toward anarchy, rather than toward democracy, could not but lead to disaster.

In December, pressure began building for me to leave the country. There had been discussions for several weeks about my taking a vacation abroad as a pre-condition for forming a coalition government; but as I have already noted, opposition leaders could not or would not agree to put the necessary procedures in place. Now foreign visitors appeared in Iran urging me to leave and to reach an accord with the opposition.

At about this time, a new CIA chief was stationed in Teheran. He had been transferred to Iran from a post in Tokyo with no previous experience in Iranian affairs. Why did the U.S. install a man totally ignorant of my country in the midst of such a crisis? I was astonished by the insignificance of the reports he gave me. At one point we spoke of liberalization and I saw a smile spread across his face. It seemed a strange interest for a high-ranking CIA official, ostensibly charged with security in the Middle East. Thus, I could only assume that his mission was to further our liberalization efforts rather than discuss security issues.

After the failure of my negotiations with Sanjabi, General Moghadam asked if I would see Mr. Shapur Bakhtiar, another member of the National Front who had served as a junior minister in the Mossadegh government. I had already had some contact with him arranged by my former prime minister, Mr. Amouzegar, who even out of office remained a trusted advisor. Unlike Sanjabi who continued to make inflammatory speeches at a time that called for calm and reason, Bakhtiar behaved in a discreet and reserved manner.

I agreed to receive him. General Moghadam brought him to the Niavaran Palace one evening. We had a lengthy conversation in which Bakhtiar profusely expressed his loyalty to the Constitution and the monarchy. He wanted to adhere to the Constitution and name a Regency Council before I left on holiday. He would seek a vote of confidence in both chambers.

It was with some reluctance and under foreign pressure that I agreed to appoint him Prime Minister. I had always considered him an Anglophile and an agent of British Petroleum. His political base lacked depth; he had admitted to me that the entire membership of the National Front consisted of only 27 people.

I finally decided to name Bakhtiar Prime Minister after my meeting with Lord George Brown, once Foreign Secretary in Britain's Labor Government. We were old friends. He took my hand and pleaded with me to leave the country. Just take a two-month vacation, he said. Then he strongly endorsed Bakhtiar. On December 29, Shahpur Bakhtiar was asked to form a civilian government.

On January 2, 1979, I made my first public appearance in two months and expressed readiness to take that much-demanded—and if truth were told much needed—holiday, once Bakhtiar's government had been confirmed and installed.

Shortly after the first of the year, General Robert Huyser, Deputy Commander of U.S. Forces in Europe, arrived unannounced in Teheran. On January 4, President Carter began the Guadaloupe meetings with French President Giscard, West German Chancellor Schmidt, and British Prime Minister Callaghan on that French-owned island in the Caribbean. Giscard said they hoped to "evaluate the situation of the world," with special emphasis on events in the eastern Mediterranean and the Persian Gulf. I believe that during those meetings the French and the West Germans agreed with the British and the American proposals for my ouster. These Guadaloupe meetings may prove to be the "Yalta of the Mideast," with the notable absence of the recipient (U.S.S.R.) of the largesse.

About the same time French President Valéry Giscard d'Estaing sent a personal envoy to Teheran, a man very close to him. He too advocated a "political" solution to the crisis, a euphemism for accommodation and abstention from the use of force. His second point, I still have difficulty understanding today: at all costs we must avoid any confrontation with the Soviet Union. I asked him what my internal affairs had to do with a confrontation between East and West, but it was a question he would not answer.

It was against this background that I learned of Huyser's mission. I had known him reasonably well. He had come to Teheran a number of times, scheduling his visits well in advance to discuss military affairs with me and my generals. I had always found him very helpful.

The unannounced visit distressed me. I asked my generals about it but they knew no more than I did. Such a man would not avoid me without good reason. As soon as Moscow learned of Huyser's arrival, *Pravda* reported: "General Huyser is in Teheran to foment a military coup." In Paris, the *International Herald Tribune* wrote that Huyser had not gone to Teheran to "foment" a coup but to "prevent" one.

Did such a risk exist? I do not believe so. My officers were tied to the Crown and the Constitution by an oath of loyalty. As long as the Constitution was respected, they would not falter.

But the different American information services had perhaps solid reasons to think that the Constitution would be abused. It was therefore necessary to neutralize the Iranian army. It was clearly for this reason that General Huyser had come to Teheran.

I saw Huyser only once. He came with Ambassador Sullivan about a week before I left Iran. Sullivan did most of the talking. The atmosphere was grim. My departure was no longer a matter of days, Sullivan said, but of hours, and looked meaningfully at his watch. Both talked of a "leave" of two months but neither seemed very convinced that I might return.

Huyser succeeded in winning over my last chief of staff, General Ghara-Baghi, whose later behavior leads me to believe that he was a traitor. He asked Ghara-Baghi to arrange a meeting for him with Mehdi Bazargan, the human-rights lawyer who became Khomeini's first Prime Minister. The General informed me of Huyser's request before I left, but I have no idea of what ensued. I do know that Ghara-Baghi used his authority to prevent military action against Khomeini. He alone knows what decisions were made and the price paid. It is perhaps significant that although all my generals were executed, only General Ghara-Baghi was spared. His savior was Mehdi Bazargan.

By the time Huyser left Iran, the army had been destroyed and the Bakhtiar government he had supposedly come to save was in shambles. At the travesty of a trial which preceded the execution of General Rabbii, the commander of the Iranian Air Force, the General told his "judges" that "General Huyser threw the Shah out of the country like a dead mouse."

Bakhtiar's government was approved by the Majlis on January 16 by a comfortable margin. Plans for my departure had been announced, interestingly enough, on January 11 in Washington by U.S. Secretary of State Vance.

Those last days were days of heartbreak, of nights without sleep, the deplorable conditions in my country were naturally my preoccupation at every moment, and it was necessary to continue to work while knowing that my departure was imminent.

I cannot nor am I willing to express fully the sentiments which I felt on January 16, 1979, when I took the road to the airport with the Empress and my children. I had in me a sinister foreboding for I knew all too well what could happen.

I wanted to persuade myself that my departure would calm the people, decrease hatred, and disarm the assassins. I hoped that Shapour Bakhtiar would perhaps be fortunate and that the country could survive, despite the immense destruction being inflicted by the furious crowd.

An icy wind, usual for this time of the year, swept the airport at Mehrabad, where rows of planes stood, immobilized by the strikes. At the foot of the plane, our national leaders were gathered to say farewell to us: Shapour Bakhtiar, the presidents of the two chambers of Parliament, ministers and generals.

I advised them all to exercise prudence. As God is my witness, I had done everything within my power to protect those who had served me.

The Imam Jom'eh who, during all my departures had been present to recite the traditional prayers, was not there. Perhaps some people misunderstood and gave his absence a significance which it did not have. The poor man was really ill and died a few weeks later in Geneva. But I had with me the copy of the Holy Koran that never leaves me.

I was completely overwhelmed by the expressions of loyalty given to me when I left. There was a poignant silence broken by sobs.

The last image which I carried of this land over which I had reigned for thirty-seven years and to which I had offered a little of my blood was that of the frightful distress on the tearful faces of those who had come to bid us farewell.

12

From Hope to Despair

My acts have often been criticized, sometimes justly. However, few of my critics have stopped to objectively evaluate the difficulties which we had to overcome. Fewer still have considered whether Iran would exist at all without the efforts which we made for her survival.

We strengthened Iran's independence and unity in 1945-46; we pulled the country out of chaos in 1953. We next put our economy and finances in order; we wrested our oil resources from foreign ownership; and from 1963 we set our people, with their overwhelming approval, upon the road of common sense and progress, toward the Great Civilization.

For 37 years all my political activities were carried out with the aim of placing my people upon the path leading to this Great Civilization. When I began my White Revolution, a shock program which would allow Iran to overcome in 25 years its centuries of suppression, I understood that its realization would not be possible except through a mobilization of all forces within the country. A permanent state of urgency was necessary if we were to prevent hostile elements from becoming stumbling blocks—elements such as reactionaries, large landowners, communists, conservatives, and international agitators. To mobilize a country, one must win it over, push it, pull it and while it is engaged in work, defend it against those who want to prevent it from working.

To let saboteurs act freely would certainly not have permitted this program's realization. Without the White Revolution, democracy in Iran would be merely a mirage, for a democracy based on hunger, ignorance, and physical and moral degeneration is but a caricature, and ultimately democracy's worst enemy.

Indeed, the road to this Great Civilization was not an easy one. But it led toward a higher standard of living. What then is this Great Civilization that I wanted for Iran? To me, it is an effort toward understanding and peace which creates the perfect environment in which everyone can work. I believe each nation has the right, the duty to reach or to return to a Great Civilization. That is why Iran cannot but be faithful to its ancestral, universalist tradition. This tradition in fact always combined certain values and a certain purely national Iranian spirit with the best available in other civilizations.

In our march toward this Great Civilization, Iran was one vast workshop in which all the elements indispensable to modernization sprang up: universities, school groups, professional institutes, hospitals, roads, railroads, dams, electric plants, pipelines for gas and oil, factories, industrial, cultural, artistic and sports complexes, cooperatives, metropolitan areas, and new villages.

When Mossadegh was in power, Iran's budget was around $400 million. Our last budget was $57 billion, of which approximately $20 billion came from oil revenues and the rest from taxes that the people could now afford; in 1963 our per capita income was $174, in 1978, the last year of my reign, it was $2,540. And all this was accomplished at a time of great population growth, from 27 million in 1968 to 36 million in 1978. And our social programs were developing under the White Revolution at a remarkable rate.

In pursuing these economic and social programs we still depended heavily on our oil revenues, which were around $22 billion in 1977. Despite our care to conserve our oil, we continued to extract five to six million barrels a day from our wells, in order to create the infrastructure which was indispensable to our development in the Twenty-first Century.

According to all forecasts, three or four years would be sufficient to fill our most important gaps. Between 1978 and 1982, our institutions of higher learning would have graduated four classes of various technicians. Steel production would have reached 10 million tons per year. I was hoping that we could later increase our level of production to 25 million tons, which is near that of France. Sixty kilometers from the Pakistani border, the vast port complex of Chahar-bahar on the Sea of Oman was nearing completion, as was the one in Bandar-Abbas on the Persian Gulf. Here ships weighing 500,000 tons could be placed on dry docks. Other large ports under construction were to have opened in 1982.

Beyond this, we planned the construction of four electro-nuclear plants, Iran I and Iran II to be built by the Germans near Bushehr and Iran III and Iran IV by the French on the Karoun River near Ahvaz. The first two were to begin to operate in 1980 and 1981 and the second two were scheduled to open at the ends of 1983 and 1984. At present, these projects have been abandoned. The sums invested have without doubt been lost without any return. Fourteen other nuclear stations were planned which would ultimately supply Iran with 25,000 megawatts of nuclear energy. A nuclear research center was planned for Isfahan.

We had also scheduled the construction of the Teheran subway, the electrification and doubling of the Teheran-Bandar Shapour railroad, and the construction of a six-lane highway along the same route.

The benefits of so many years of effort are now reduced to nothing. Our oil production is far from having regained its former momentum and—it has been declared in Teheran—it never will. The wells are managed by incompetent people, perhaps untrained workers, and oil exploitation is carried out so poorly that some wells have already been ruined.

The Communists and their allies have gradually seized the workers' and peasants' organizations. It is, moreover, the rank and file who give orders, dismiss or appoint directors, engineers, and supervisors. They make decisions about production and vote themselves enormous salary increases.

Since it has been forbidden to fire any employee of a business, sabotage can only be prevented by closing down plants or by "nationalization," which means allowing the nation to pay for a deficit made greater by a myriad of new bureaucracies, incompetence, and corruption. In certain cases the owners themselves have asked for "nationalization."

During the summer of 1979 the industrial infrastructure of the country practically collapsed as a result of all this—notably the large steel, copper, and aluminum industries, mines, docks, and car and tractor manufacturers. Before they disappear forever, these industries will cost the taxpayers a great deal.

Most factories lack both orders and primary materials, and can operate at only 25-30 percent capacity while they await the closing of their doors. Needless to say, the workers have lost all the advantages which the White Revolution bestowed upon them. Besides, there is nothing left to share. The working classes have indeed been profoundly hurt by the "Islamic Revolution." It was made against their interests. I had given the greatest possible number of citizens the power to rise and free themselves from proletarian conditions. It is with despair that I see workers, peasants, and employees without work, falling again into financial difficulty and sometimes into misery.

The rapid depreciation of money and galloping inflation make it practically impossible to establish reasonable programs of production even on a short-term basis. The net cost of a manufactured object is impossible to ascertain.

In public works and construction, stagnation has been the rule since the winter of 1979. The State has renounced almost all the major projects, and the multinational enterprises do not want to carry out any activity under a regime which has cancelled past orders without paying the contractual penalties.

Of the 180 French firms which were working in Iran in 1978, I understand that half had already withdrawn by March 1979. All the foreign firms that remained have had to work under very difficult conditions, the enterprises having to receive "revolutionary committees" with claims that are impossible to satisfy.

The new Iranian authorities let it be known that the indemnities for broken contracts would not be paid to foreigners. Revolution and change of regime now fall under the category of "unforeseen circumstances which are an absolute necessity."

The present political and religious chaos and xenophobia are no less costly to American, German, Italian, Japanese, and other firms which have lost important orders for materials or work. Dupont de Nemours (U.S.A.) and Mitsubishi (Japan) invested and lost considerable capital in our country. The greatest loser is the United States. We signed a commercial treaty with the United States which foresaw their selling us ten billion dollars of materials and equipment during a five year period. It is now defunct.

The moral aspect of this catastrophe is no less grave. The consequences of the bloody fiasco of Khomeini may prove to be disastrous for Islam in general and Shi'ism in particular. The megalomania of the troubled mind of Qom and the dictatorship of a band of mullahs are in formal contradiction to the essential principles of Islam. History will reveal how a head of state anxious about the future of his people, a man calling for solidarity among other peoples, was to be ostracized. My exile has permitted, or will permit, certain people to take up the so-called policy of expensive oil for their own benefit and to their own profit.

My disappearance from the world political and economic scene has coincided with a general offensive against the economic and even political stability of Western powers. This crisis, moreover, is only one of several means employed to destabilize not only the Middle East but the world economy.

It is said that today the events in Iran have altered the rapport of world forces. It is said that "times have changed" and that the common man or citizen "has to adapt himself to the new state of the world." I am afraid that signifies he must adapt himself to chaos.

13

The Terror

THOSE WHO "GOVERN" IN Teheran since my departure have demonstrated their impotence and irresponsibility. Shapour Bakhtiar wanted to govern, but could not. Mehdi Bazargan, the pseudo-prime minister of the so-called Islamic Republic, never governed over anything, for Iran no longer had a constitution or a parliament. He was a chameleon who consented, contradicted, and retracted any and all of his policies to please the mullahs and their advisors, ignoring the needs of our nation and its people.

On January 23, 1979, Mr. Bazargan declared, "The Islamic Republic which we shall proclaim will not resemble Libya or Saudi Arabia, but rather the Islamic government which existed during the first years of the Caliphate Ali'." On March 30-31, a pseudo-referendum was organized to put the Islamic Republic to a popular vote. It was a grotesque farce. People over the age of 15 voted. A green ballot meant a vote for the "Islamic Republic" and a red indicated a no-vote. Since this public election was held under the surveillance of the Guards of the Revolution, is it surprising that 98 percent of the voters cast green ballots? The Iranian media announced that the "Islamic Republic" had been voted on by approximately 23 million Iranians. But half of our population, nearly 18 million people, is under 15 years of age. Even if one assumes that everyone voted, that would make at least 5 million votes too many. This republic was declared on April 1, 1979, and Iran thereby returned to the Middle Ages.

Ironically, Mr. Bazargan, who was the former president of the Association for Human Rights, now presided over a reign of terror. What mockery that these executioners pretend to render justice "in the name of God." This blind fanaticism has established in our country a reign of terror, folly, and stupidity.

What is difficult to understand is the Western media's double standard—my government was continually characterized as a tyrannical, repressive regime which trampled on Iranians' freedoms and liberties, but Khomeini's government seems to be glorified by some as a new revolution. Since many earlier revolutions have freed the oppressed, I feel that perhaps it is difficult for the Western mind to face the reality that revolution is not always a positive force for mankind. Neither Castro's Cuba nor Khomeini's regime have freed their peoples. Moreover, those international human rights agencies which at one time gave us so much good advice on humanizing our criminal justice system appear to have melted away with the advent of this so-called Islamic Republic.

In this republic's inquisitional process, the essential accusation remains irrefutable. The prisoners are accused of being "corrupters of the earth." This does not at all signify, as certain Western reporters seem to think, that the accused have permitted themselves to be corrupted by bribes, nor does it mean that they were accused of betrayal of trust, thievery, or any other peculation. The term "corrupter of the earth" is an expression from the Koran which denotes all individuals whose iniquities, vices, and sins offend God.

No penal code in the world has employed such a vague expression to define an offense or a crime. It is obvious that one can be a "corrupter of the earth" in the eyes of inquisitors for numerous reasons. The accused is proclaimed *ipso facto* to be impure before God and from that moment must be removed from the earth which he blemishes.

The "Islamic Tribunals" disdain the most elementary rights of defense. In the minds of the religious "judges," the accused are obvious criminals solely because they participated in the political, social, and economic life of Iran during my reign. Those who naively protest their innocence and observe that during all this time of corruption the mullahs also lived very well, only succeed in aggravating their cases. To offer testimony and pleadings before these tribunals is useless.

At the beginning of February 1979, Bazargan promised that the politically accused "would be judged publicly by regular tribunals" and declared himself to be fiercely opposed to an "expeditious procedure." A few days later General Nematollah Nassiri, who had been the head of the State Security, was removed by the militia from the prison where he was awaiting trial. Beaten and tortured, he appeared during the evening of February 12 before television cameras, his face swollen, covered with bandages, hardly able to express himself. However, he did speak and in the midst of his executioners, declared that he had not ordered any murders and that he had never received any orders to torture prisoners. The Committee shot him during the early morning hours of February 16 along with three other generals who proclaimed their faithfulness to Iran and their sovereign.

On February 28 Bazargan threatened to resign if the discretionary powers of the committees were not defined and limited. On March 8, "firm assurances" were given to him on this subject. But in fact arrests, followed by firing squads and summary executions, doubled. Almost all the generals who were division commanders were put to death because they had committed the crime of exercising command under my reign. A senator who was more than a hundred years old was executed because of his fidelity to the monarchy and a number of accused who were more than seventy years old were also killed. Everyone was guilty; everyone was a potential victim. Among the published names of the assassinated were ministers and secretaries of state, diplomats, parliamentarians, governors of provinces, mayors and municipal counsellors, numerous generals and officers from the army, junior officers, ordinary soldiers, police officers and officers of state police, journalists, editors and radio reporters, magistrates, lawyers, religious authorities, doctors, professors, sports figures, and businessmen. All were condemned and received summary executions "in the name of God."

Thousands of citizens escaped by fleeing Iran, as did Shapour Bakhtiar. Since February 1979 even some religious authorities have been assassinated and persecuted. Until now the terror exercised by the militia has prevented certain ayatollahs from publicly declaring their severe judgment of the massacres ordered by the so-called Islamic tribunals. During revolutionary torments the vast number of those terrorized follow the ringleader. In *Le Monde* on March 8, 1979, an "open letter" to Khomeini was published by Bakhtiar's son, which said in part:

"You need heads, Mr. Khomeini, and at this hour when I cry out, many have already fallen, through your divine will, without knowing at all exactly what their count of indictment was.... But under what name do you qualify, you who through cassettes sent by intermediaries have sent thousands of fanaticized young people joyfully to their deaths?

"Do not hope for history to flatter you. You have prevented Iran from attaining its chance for democracy. And you are responsible for too many martyrs to ever become a hero."

This letter was written before the militias of the so-called Islamic Revolution had become tightly organized. Many "suspects," especially in the provinces, could still escape the raids of the vigilantes who provided the "Islamic tribunals" with fodder, or indulged in summary executions followed by pillaging.

These gangs multiplied during January and February when the insurrectionists stripped the barracks and arsenals. To my knowledge they never returned their arms. The best known and the most powerful of these vigilantes are the "Revolutionary Committees" which have at least ten thousand active militants about whom nothing is known. One such group, the "Guardians of the Revolution" is a paramilitary organization founded by Ibrahim Yazdi, the famous advisor at Neauphle-le-Château—a peculiar figure who traveled with an American passport and became Bazargan's deputy and foreign minister.

During this terrible month of March many other innocent people were "judged" and executed. The executed had no knowledge of the accusations made against them; they had no time to prepare their defense; no lawyer; a trial behind closed doors; anonymous judges—these were the innovations of so-called Islamic justice.

On March 11, the speaker for the Bazargan cabinet, Amir Entezam, declared to the press: "The government in general and the Ministry of Justice in particular cannot exercise any control upon the deliberations and decisions of the Islamic revolutionary tribunals."

Once more Bazargan threatened to resign. But he remained. On March 16, Bazargan had asked for a suspension of the trial of Amir Abbas Hoveyda, who had been my Prime Minister for thirteen years. This man of rare merit had but one fault: his extreme courage carried him to temerity.

Here I want to make certain clarifications which seem to me to be necessary. During the fall of 1978, the most diverse methods were employed to accuse the administration. Amir Abbas Hoveyda served as the scapegoat.

A very clever intrigue was mounted, and Hoveyda, whose frankness and loyalty were known to me, did not perceive the dangers which threatened him personally. Hoveyda was promised a fair trial with all the constitutional and legal guarantees which would have justified him and others who had long been a part of his government. He was not afraid of a just trial.

Arrested on November 8, 1978, he was freed from his prison by the riots a few months later. Instead of escaping, he went to the house of a friend where he telephoned the Committee in order to inform them of his whereabouts. They returned him to prison where he undertook to prepare a statement in his defense.

However, his inquisitors refused to let him finish his defense. He was grossly mistreated. Men who had seen him before his reimprisonment said he appeared to have lost more than 40 pounds. At dawn on Thursday, March 15, he was taken before a self-styled "revolutionary tribunal" and condemned to death without any opportunity to defend himself against their charges. When accused of having "battled against God," he reproached his anonymous judges in these terms: "I did not ever declare war against God—how could I have done so?—I am a believer and have gone to Mecca. If you have decided that I am guilty, then I am so. Do what is necessary. But here we all lived under the same laws, the same system of government.... All our laws were promulgated by the parliament and each person approved it."

On the evening of April 7, an executioner killed Amir Abbas Hoveyda with a burst of machine gun fire. But it seems that he was already dying from the ill-treatment he had received.

When I heard of his execution, I shut myself up for a whole day and prayed. Hoveyda's death had been an assassination. It could not be disguised or ignored, and a real cry of horror and indignation arose from the press in the free world. The governments of the West officially expressed "their emotion, consternation and grave concern." At the United Nations, Mr. Kurt Waldheim could not but note the "indifference with which the new Iranian authorities have confronted the calls for mercy and justice."

Meanwhile the executioners continued their work. At two o'clock in the morning of April 11, a "tribunal" condemned eleven officials to death, after a brief deliberation. They were assassinated half an hour later. The first of these victims was General Hassan Pakravan. His sole "crime" was to have headed SAVAK fifteen years earlier. He had a reputation for probity and goodness. He had often appealed to me on behalf of opponents sentenced by our courts and particularly on behalf of numerous mullahs. Four generals were executed with him.

The International Commission of Jurists, in Geneva noted that the "Islamic tribunals" which judged and condemned in Iran "deliberately violated the international conventions of the United Nations concerning civil and political rights, conventions which Iran had signed."

Mr. Khomeini's response was brief. From Qom on May 4, he declared: "The Revolution must cut the hands of the rotten. . . . Blood must be spilled. The more Iran bleeds, the more will the Revolution be victorious."

In late February, the committees of the Military Wing of the Revolution had decreed "the complete renovation of the Army." This meant that a veritable popular army was to be achieved through the elimination of commanders with too well-known backgrounds. From February until June the violent repression continued but in a more organized manner. During this period more than twenty generals, superior officers of the general staff, colonels as well as air force and naval officers, were assassinated. On May 8 in Teheran, following a summary trial, the "Guardians of the Revolution" killed 21 people. This group of victims included political as well as military figures.

On May 10, General Fazollah Nazimi, who had commanded a brigade of the Iron Guards, was killed. Later "the great burning" took place in Kerman. In a helter-skelter fashion, officers, gypsies, and women were condemned. One hundred fourteen people were found "corrupt." Assassinations of generals, colonels, battallion commanders, and officers of the state police continued until mid-June. In addition, some 250 officers of the general staff or superiors of the different forces were imprisoned, transferred, or dismissed. In this way, the Army lost its leadership.

At the beginning of September, the international press published the names of some 575 people officially executed since February 16, by decree of so-called Islamic tribunals. No communist leader was on this casualty list. The press, however, appeared not to have noticed this detail. Khomeini's tribunals assassinated only true believers, "in the name of God." Victims of guerilla groups and militia bands who roamed the provinces remain unaccounted. These insurgents had stripped our arsenals in early January; they killed and pillaged with impunity in Teheran as well as the provinces.

At the end of March the "Guardians of the Revolution" had arrested and imprisoned Amir Hossein Atapour, a 78-year-old retired general. His son, Fariborz Atapour, was an editor of the *Teheran Journal* and wrote a courageous article in which he revealed that *"at least twenty thousand political detainees are stagnating in improvised jails and prisons."* Why are these horrors passed over in silence, ignored by the world? During my reign there were never more than 3,200 so-called political detainees, and most of these were in fact terrorists. Since February, it is certain that many tens of thousands of men and women have been and are being arrested and imprisoned, frequently under inhuman conditions. They have sometimes been beaten or tortured. The number of people who have died in prison is also unknown.

During my reign, members of the International Red Cross could visit freely all the penitentiaries of the country. Our prisons remained open to all qualified investigators. The lawyer of every detainee had knowledge of the file of the accused and time to prepare his defense and to summon the necessary witnesses. Finally, the condemned could make an appeal and seek an annulment, after which I often exercised my right of pardon. This is no longer the case. These so-called Islamic tribunals are an insult to the exalted principles of the Holy Koran.

That spring the International Red Cross was forbidden to visit or aid any prisoners. On April 1, Mr. Khomeini alluded to the fate of the innumerable men and women who had been imprisoned. I quote: "All these people should have been killed from the first days instead of crowding the prisons. It is not a question of people who are accused but of criminals. Only those who were notorious criminals were killed and now we judge these people according to documents whereas they should not be judged but killed. It is deplorable to acknowledge to what an extent Westernization rages still among us."

On May 13, the Agence France-Presse sent this dispatch: "Teheran. The Ayatollah Khomeini has addressed a message to President Giscard d'Estaing to thank 'his French friends' for their welcome but deplores the fact that they throw human rights in his face for a few criminals and thieves."

I was astounded to learn that Andrew Young, defender of human rights, had declared the author of this barbarism a "saint."

And what of the so-called Islamic Constitution which institutionalizes clerical supremacy? Its critical feature is the supreme power it gives to its leader, which parallels the "führer" principle. Why is this ignored? In terms of human rights, this constitution severely limits freedom of speech, assembly, and press. Where are the human rights advocates now? The duly elected Bani Sadr actually sits only at the pleasure of the leader, currently Mr. Khomeini, for under this Islamic Constitution Iran's new führer has the power to suspend the president at any time.

What is more, this so-called Islamic Revolution, through its medieval methods of public torture and death, is brutalizing its populace. And what can I say about Khomeini's seizure of over 50 innocent Americans on November 4, 1979, in their own embassy? He leads the people into a daily deification of terrorism.

This so-called "saint" succeeded in bringing Iran to its knees. The very fabric of our nation is in ruins as a result of Khomeini's theocracy, which affords the government almost limitless powers over all aspects of Iranian life. The popular despair his reign of terror and stupidity created can only lead to communism.

14

Conclusions

IRAN IS PREY TO a counterrevolution whose proclaimed goal is to annihilate all that our White Revolution accomplished.

Five centuries after the Spanish Inquisition, Iran lives under the terror of its own Torquemada—one far more merciless. The fact is that people condemned by the Spanish Inquisition were spared if they repented. They could offer witnesses in their own behalf, a privilege denied by the Iranian Torquemada.

Hatred, vengeance, and massacre can never serve the cause of Islam, whose tenets teach justice, goodness, forgiveness, and high morals. Thus, this explosion of hatred, unleashed supposedly in the "name of God," is an insult to God and to our religion. And this insult, I repeat, risks great wrong to Islam, as the Inquisition once wronged Catholicism.

For myself, I have always believed that real faith consists in respecting and following the spirit and soul of a religion, not in remaining the prisoner of a sectarian dogmatism. It is not in closing mixed schools, condemning women to wear the veil or to share their married life with another woman while depriving them of the right of divorce accorded their husbands; it is not by bringing women to an inferior condition that the spirit of Islam is served. On the contrary, it is in emancipating women, in giving them all the possibilities of education, in assuring them the highest dignity possible, and in providing them a state of complete equality with men in all fields that the truths of the Koran find expression.

Is it conceivable for a human being worthy of this name to flog, stone, or cut off the hand of the wrongdoer on the pretext that these punishments were given under the caliphs in the Middle Ages? To combat evil where evil exists, in the purest spirit of Islam, is to educate, to foster goodness, and to pardon.

The Iranian flag, which does not date from our dynasty, under whose folds millions of Iranians have sacrificed themselves during many centuries, is despised by the leaders of this so-called revolution. The kings who led Persia through triumphs and trials in one of the most beautiful of the histories of the civilized world now stand cursed by the moguls of Qom. This obliteration of our national identity and the cultural and spiritual heritage of Iran is abhorrent. Our identity and heritage are our greatest advantages, the essential foundations from which everything else can be recovered and without which all will be lost.

Today, our Great Civilization may appear to have died for all time. I believe, however, that like those powerful rivers that disappear underneath the mountains, lost to view, only to emerge later in full force, Persian culture will rise to the surface again, nourished by the values, creations, thought, talent, and effort of the people. From their trials will be reborn both spiritual and material victories.

Let us not forget that the Iranians who were living at the time of the Holy Prophet's birth were praised by him as those who "searched for the Truth." I have sincerely sought the truth for myself and for my nation. Under my reign Iranians were not searching after falsehoods.

My thoughts have never left my country. They remain there. I think of all those compatriots who, under the reign of my father and myself, pulled Iran out of darkness and servitude and transformed it into the great nation it was in 1978. Today, away from our country, I prove my gratitude to them by but a single means, yet one which I believe firmly to be the most powerful of all—prayer.

I pray for those in the agony of poverty and death.

I pray for our youth, deceived and misguided.

I pray for those who suffer in silence.

I pray for those who are hunted and slandered.

I pray for those who remain blind to falsehood and deceit. May God enlighten them and remove hate forever from their hearts.

O God Almighty, in Whom I have believed all my life, preserve our country and save our people.

Appendix I

Principles of Iran's White Revolution

Item	Date
The original six points:	Announced by the Shah, January 9, 1963, and endorsed by national referendum, January 26, 1963
1. Land reform (detailed in the 1962 land reform law)	
2. Nationalization of forests	
3. Sale of state-owned enterprises to the public	
4. Workers' profit-sharing in 20 percent of net corporate earnings	
5. Voting and political rights for women	
6. Formation of the Literacy Corps	
Additional three points, 1964-65	
7. Formation of the Health Corps	January 21, 1964
8. Formation of the Reconstruction and Development Corps	September 23, 1964
9. Establishment of Houses of Equity	October 13, 1965
Additional three points, 1967	October 6, 1967
10. Program for nationalization of water resources	
11. Program for urban and rural reconstruction	
12. Administrative revolution (modernization, decentralization)	
Additional five points, 1975	
13. Employee and public ownership extension scheme (up to 99 percent in state-owned enterprises and 49 percent in private firms)	September 9, 1975

14. Price stabilization and campaign against profiteering	September 9, 1975
15. Free education and a daily free meal for all children from kindergarten to eighth grade	mid-December 1975
16. Free nutrition for infants up to the age of two	late December 1975
17. Nation-wide social security (to be extended to rural population)	late December 1975
18. Fight against land & housing speculation	
19. Fight against corruption	

TAKEN FROM: *Iran Under the Pahlavis,* George Lenczowski, ed. Hoover Institution Press: 1978. Reprinted by permission.

SOURCES: *Area Handbook for Iran,* American University, Foreign Area Studies, 1971; Mohammad Reza Shah Pahlavi, *The White Revolution,* Tehran: 1967; *Kayhan International; Quarterly Economic Review.*

Appendix II

National Health Organizations

These organizations, not referred to in the text, were particularly active in protecting national health.

The Charitable Society of Farah Pahlavi
The Charitable Foundation of the Queen Mother
The Charitable Foundation of Shams Pahlavi
The Charitable Foundation of Ashraf Pahlavi
National Organization for Assistance to the Blind and the Deaf
National Organization for the Welfare of Families
National Society for the Protection of Children
National Society for Orphans
National Society for the Deaf and Dumb
National Society for the Paralyzed
Society for Aid to Lepers
Society for the Protection of Tuberculosis Patients
Society for the Fight Against Cancer
National Blood Organization
The Hospital for Heart Diseases

The Hospital for Heart Diseases was founded by my mother and was known as one of the best cardiological centers in the world. All of these organizations collaborated with the ministers who had jurisdiction in their field of work.

Appendix III

Iranian Armed Forces: 1982

By 1982 our armies would have increased from 540,000 men to 760,000. The following summary will give an idea of how our strength was distributed.

Tanks

1,500 "Lions of Iran." Specially designed for us by British engineers, this tank is equal, if not superior to all others because of its new engine, its 120mm gun, its laser-beam range-finder and new armor-plating.

800 "Chieftain" tanks with an improved engine, fitted with the same cannon and the same firing quipment.

406 M-60 modernized tanks (U.S.) with a 105 mm gyroscopic gun.

400 modernized M-47s, with a 90mm gun which could be replaced by a 105mm.

250 "Scorpion" reconnaissance tanks. Other tanks of this variety were due to be ordered in the meantime.

Besides a thousand armored troop-transporters and armored mobile-control posts mounted on American M113 chassis, we had 2,000 Russian-made armored troop-transporters on tracks and on wheels. They are the best of their kind. Many of them would have had, in addition, a 73mm gun and anti-tank missiles.

Artillery

In principle our artillery batallions were to have the same firing strength as NATO artillery. By 1982, our armament factories would have produced 105mm, 120mm, and 150mm cannons and more.

Air Force

78 F14s with Phoenix missiles having a 90-mile range, and 150-mile range radar equipment, and able to fire six missiles at different targets at the same time.

250 regularly modernized "Phantoms"; the oldest of these having laser bombs; and the most modern with a "black box" capable of warding off enemy missiles.

Over 100 F5Es

About 100 F14s (or F15s, depending on which the Americans decided to build).

106 F16s already ordered. We were negotiating to order an additional 140.

7 airborne radar systems, reaching to at least 35,000 feet, which would have meant that we could economize on 30 ground systems; and other airborne electronic look-out devices.

24 modernized 747 and 707 air-tankers capable of refueling each other. We had had this air-tanker modified according to my own plans. This fleet would have allowed us to keep the maximum amount of airplanes airborne and would have saved time. We were going to order at least another twelve.

57 military transporters of the C130 "Hercules" variety, with propellors.

Besides these, some of our factories which were working on behalf of national defense were ready to manufacture:

Anti-aircraft missiles of the SAM 7 type (U.S.S.R.).

Air-to-ground "Maverick" missiles (U.S.) with extremely precise homing devices reaching as far as twelve miles. I am told that the factory at Shiraz where the "Mavericks" and TOWs would have been built has been destroyed.

Anti-tank TOW missiles. We thought that we would surpass the Americans and change from the sub-sonic radio-controlled TOW to supersonic laser team TOW.

Anti-tank rockets (U.S.S.R.).

"Dragon" radio-controlled rocket launchers (U.S.) for the infantry. They would have twice the usual range—i.e., 1,000 instead of 500 meters.

Several hundred "Oerlimpon" anti-aircraft guns.

We were also developing a new twin barrel 35mm anti-aircraft gun which was better and simpler.

In addition to this 35mm gun, we were also developing a 20mm anti-aircraft gun.

100 "Rapier" anti-aircraft missiles, both towed and selfpropelled. We had the capability to manufacture these in our own country.

We already had three airborne brigades and, by 1982, we would have had five, which meant more than a division.

The Navy

Our expectations were as follows:

Four 8,000-ton cruisers, standard sea-to-air missile launchers with a speed of Mach 3, and sea-to-sea "Harpoons" with a subsonic speed whose normal range would have been increased from 90 to 150 kilometres thanks to a relay helicopter. We were also planning to make the "Harpoons" supersonic, and a submarine launch was under study.

Twelve 3,000-ton destroyers armed with standard "Harpoons" ordered from Holland and Germany.

12 "Combattant IIs" (France).

3 U.S. submarines, already ordered.

9 submarines to be ordered from Europe, probably from West Germany.

50 naval helicopters.

A fleet of troop ships, tankers, supply ships. This naval force could have not only cruised in the Gulf, but could have reached the farthest shores of the Indian Ocean.

Some "Orion" (Lockheed) long-range reconnaissance planes which would have been used by the navy while remaining answerable to the Air Force.

Index